TWAYNE'S WORLD AUTHORS SERIES

A Survey of the World's Literature

Sylvia E. Bowman, Indiana University
GENERAL EDITOR

CHINA

Howard S. Levy, Tokyo
and
William R. Schultz, University of Arizona
EDITORS

Tu Fu

(TWAS 110)

詩聖杜拾遺像

TU FU

Tu Fu

By A. R. DAVIS

University of Sydney

Twayne Publishers, Inc.   ::   New York

To My Wife

Preface

The present Tu Fu's Thatched Hut at Ch'eng-tu is reported to contain more than twenty different portraits of the poet, painted from the Yüan (1280-1367) period onwards. This among the many statistics which might be quoted about Tu Fu, who had a greater influence than any other poet on the generations that followed him, provides the best excuse for this little book. All these portraits are imaginary, though some may have been influenced by others, just as what I have written has been influenced by others' writing and especially by Professor William Hung's invaluable book, *Tu Fu: China's Greatest Poet*. But their final source is Tu Fu's poetry and this has been my basic material.

Compared with many other Chinese poets, Tu Fu's work is rich in biographical detail, and he has been studied by many more commentators over the centuries than any other poet. This may lead to a feeling that our knowledge of Tu Fu is more intimate and more "objective" than it really is. In fact, almost all the resources of a modern contemporary biography are lacking and the man is seen through the individual scholar's subjective response to Tu Fu's self-image, created in his poetry.

I have tried here to set the emphasis on Tu Fu as a poet without suspending my judgment of him as a man. To a great extent I have avoided the smaller details of his biography and the aspect of him as an historian of his times, which has been very thoroughly treated in Professor Hung's book. Thus, although my first three chapters trace his life, they follow a possible division of his poetic career. The chapters of the second part have been devised to provide a means of looking at more of his poetry in a different manner.

Without exaggeration of the difficulty of the task, it must be said that to write of Tu Fu for the general reader and to provide translations which in any way justify the greatness claimed for him is not easy. Some 1450 of his poems survive; many are by Chinese standards long; many are hard to read, as Chinese themselves have complained for centuries, and require extensive annotation. For my illustrations I have mainly chosen from the simpler and more popular poems, but even these often contain matter for explanation. Sometimes I have contrived some explanation in introducing the poem, sometimes added it in parentheses at the end of the translation, and in other cases relegated it to the notes at the end of the book. In these devices I have tried to consider the general reader; from a Sinological standpoint my annotation is abbreviated. What I have generally avoided is the practice of substituting and dissolving away difficult reference in the course of translation. This smoothing technique seems to me calculated to destroy the character of any poetry. Though my translations are rather rough to the ear, I hope to carry over some of the style as well as the sense of the original. I have not hesitated to give partial translations in the case of some of the long poems or where a complete translation might bring in unwarranted obscurities needing long explanation. Finally, in the mildly technical chapter on forms I have tried to confine myself to what I hope can be discerned through the medium of translation and avoided that which requires a knowledge of Chinese.

My warmest acknowledgement goes to Professor Hung's work, which places anyone who follows him in something of a dilemma. I could have given a formal reference to his book in the great majority of my notes or followed the doubtful course of reference in the minority of cases where we differ. Generally I have done neither. I can only hope that my emphasis will seem sufficiently different to justify my treading in his tracks. Secondly, I am grateful for the existence of Erwin von Zach's complete German translation of the poems. Only when one has attempted to translate a substantial number of Tu Fu's poems does one begin properly to appreciate the magnitude of von Zach's achievement and the high standard it maintains. The biography by the modern Chinese poet Feng Chih was often helpful to me, as were many of the other modern Chinese and Japanese works listed in the bibliography. My regret is that time has prevented my making full use of the wealth of Tu Fu studies which might have caused me to modify some thoughts. In the end, however, like the twenty or so portraitists, one has to follow one's individual vision of a Tu Fu.

A. R. Davis

Contents

Preface

Chronology   11

1. The Formative Years   13

2. The Essential Years   45

3. The Years of Fullness   67

4. Tu Fu and Poetry   98

5. The Forms of Tu Fu's Poetry   107

6. Some Themes in Tu Fu's Poetry   128

7. By Way of Conclusion: Values and Influence   150

   Notes and References   155

   Selected Bibliography   165

   Index   168

Chronology

712 Born.

731 Begins his travels in "Wu and Yüeh" (Kiangsu, Chekiang).

736 Takes the literary examination in Ch'ang-an and fails.

740 His father Tu Hsien dies (?).

742 Takes up residence in Lo-yang.

744 Makes excursions with Li Po and Kao Shih.

746 Returns to Ch'ang-an.

747 Attempts the special examination. No candidates pass.

748 Seeks Wei Chi's help to secure a post.

750 His patron Li Chin, Prince of Ju-yang, dies.

754 Moves his family to Feng-hsien in autumn.

755 Returns to Ch'ang-an and receives an official appointment. Returns again to Feng-hsien.

756 An Lu-shan rebellion forces him to flee with his family. Captured by rebels and taken to Ch'ang-an.

757 Escapes from Ch'ang-an to the imperial court. Appointed an Omissioner.

759 Goes on a mission to Lo-yang; later gives up his post and goes to Ch'eng-tu.

760 Builds the Thatched Hut.

762 Revolt in Ch'eng-tu; flees from Mien-chou to Tzu-chou.

763 End of An-Shih rebellion.

764 Plans to return home, but returns to the Thatched Hut. Becomes a military adviser to Yen Wu.

765 Resigns post as military adviser. Falls ill at Yün-an.

766 Leaves Yün-an in spring for K'uei-chou.

768 Visits Chiang-ling and Kung-an.

769 Travels to Yüeh-chou, Heng-chou, and T'an-chou.

770 Flees in May from a local revolt in T'an-chou; returns and dies in the winter.

CHAPTER 1

The Formative Years

I A *Literary Childhood*

> By my seventh year my thoughts were already bold;
> With my opening notes I sang of the phoenix.
> By my ninth year I wrote large characters;
> My compositions quite filled a bag.[1]

TU FU gave just fourteen lines to his boyhood in his long auto-biographical poem, *The Wanderings of My Prime*. He left no poem tracing his ancestors back to the emperors or ministers of highest (and most doubtful) antiquity, as some earlier famous poets had done. That valued source, a tomb inscription, which, like a modern newspaper obituary, mixed basic biographical details with expressions of praise, was not written for Tu Fu until 813, more than forty years after his death. Though then written by Yüan Chen (779–831), himself a major poet, this tomb inscription—forty years is a long time—is thin in its biographical information. Tu Fu's own funerary writings provide a few more clues to his family and his childhood, but sufficient puzzles were left to exercise scholars over the past thousand years, often without final agreement, until the present day. Some details which have been extensively argued are matters of pedantic satisfaction rather than of intrinsic importance; much that could be valuable to know of Tu Fu's early life is unknowable.

He was born in 712, a thirteenth-generation descendant of Tu Yü (222–84), known both for his commentary to one of the most important Confucian canonical books, the history *Tso-chuan*, and as a general. Tu Fu wrote a ceremonial piece for this remote ancestor on the occasion of offering sacrifice at his tomb in 741. To have been conscious of being the descendant of the author of a standard commentary to one of the prescribed books for the examinations which gave entry into government service *and* a man remembered as a general was of some significance in Tu Fu's life. He was the most erudite of poets, was to be called the "poet-historian," and clearly saw himself as a military tactician.

The intervening generations between Tu Yü in the third century and his grandfather Tu Shen-yen (d.708) seem to have been known only vaguely to Tu Fu as maintaining a tradition of Confucianism and public office. There were no great names so that one may suppose the men not to have been very real to him. His grandfather, however, had in his day enjoyed a reputation as a prose writer and also a poet. Some forty of his poems survived for inclusion in the *Complete Poems of T'ang,* compiled early in the eighteenth century[2]. His grandfather's literary reputation must have been an encouragement to Tu Fu as a young man. As a boy, we may imagine him pouring over his grandfather's works. There are a few cases of possible reminiscence of Shen-yen's poems in his grandson's poetry and there could have been others for which the evidence no longer remains. By the time he came in his later years to associate himself with Shen-yen in a family tradition of poetry he would have realized that he himself was the significant contributor to the tradition. Tu Shen-yen was, after all, a minor poet who gained some reflected glory from his grandson.

Scholarly speculation surrounds Tu Fu's parents. He mentions his father Tu Hsien as deceased in the tomb inscription for his step-grandmother (Shen-yen married twice) in 744, and he writes in a poem of going to pay his respects to his father (probably after his failure in the examinations of 736) at Yen-chou (modern Tzu-yang hsien, Shantung), where Hsien was an assistant prefect. His father finds no other mention in his poetry, probably mainly because all the surviving poems date from after Hsien's death. Hsien seems to have held two other provincial posts before his last appointment at Yen-chou, but he remains only a shadow. Tu Fu's mother, who does not appear in his works, must have died soon after his birth. His three brothers and a sister, who were often in his thoughts and in his poetry in later life, were the children of Tu Hsien's second wife.

Apart from his early loss of her, one other fact is known about Tu Fu's mother: she was born a Ts'ui, since his maternal grandfather was a member of this wealthy and important clan. The Ts'uis intermarried with the imperial Li clan and Tu Fu was descended through his mother from the great expansionist emperor, T'ai-tsung (reigned 627–649). His relatives, Tus, Lis, Ts'uis and other maternal connections, were important to Tu Fu in a quite practical way throughout much of his life, since he often had to look to them for support.

The district in which Tu Fu's family had been formally registered seems to have been Tu-ling in the capital prefecture of Ching-chao. He was presented as a candidate for the examination of 736 by the prefect of Ching-chao, and he often gives himself the designation "of Tu-ling." It was in Tu Village he lived for a time during the 750's as a family elder. There is no way of knowing whether he was born in this area just south of Ch'ang-an, then the world's greatest city, or elsewhere. Some of his boyhood —again how much cannot be known—was spent in the eastern capital, Lo-yang, which was not far behind Ch'ang-an in size and magnificence. For we know that as a small child he was in the care of his aunt, married to an official named P'ei Jung-chi. He believed that he owed this aunt his life. In her tomb inscription he describes how, when he and his aunt's son were both lying ill, she moved him to her son's place in the southwest corner of the house, which a shamaness had declared to be favorable; her son died and Tu Fu survived.

Tu Fu's birth almost coincided with the beginning of the reign of Emperor Hsüan-tsung, the formal commencement of which is dated from 713. The reign of Hsüan-tsung began with China at a high point of territorial expansion and military power. Early eighth-century China may be described in terms of social and political organization and of material prosperity as the most advanced country in the world of that time.

She had been reunified in 589, after nearly three centuries of division, by the short-lived Sui dynasty. Under the Sui, control had been re-established over Tongking in the south, and China had again become a power in central Asia. Internally, the Sui had created or re-created governmental institutions, which their successors continued and developed, and had made a major improvement in the empire's communications by the construction of the Grand Canal, linking the area southeast of the Yangtse with north China. The Yang house of Sui was overthrown by the Li house of T'ang in 618. The second emperor, T'ai-tsung, broke Turkish power in central Asia and pushed Chinese suzerainty beyond the Pamirs. Korea and Tibet also became Chinese vassals in the seventh century.

After the expansion of the preceding century, Hsüan-tsung's reign was to be the apogee of T'ang cultural brilliance—the High-T'ang period of Chinese poetry. The exotic and the strange poured in from countries near and far, and all the arts, not merely poetry, flourished. The long reign of Hsüan-tsung was, however, amid all its splendor to witness the gradual rise of destructive political, military, and economic forces, and was to end in the great rebellion of An Lu-shan in 755. The dynasty was restored and survived until 907, but never regained its power beyond China proper, nor indeed was again complete master within those limits.

It was the crash of Hsüan-tsung's state as much as its glory that made Tu Fu a great poet. His childish claims to fame are not too exceptional. Many similar statements of youthful prodigy as his filling a bag with compositions at the age of eight can be found. He wrote also in *The Wanderings of My Prime*:

> In the past in my fourteenth or fifteenth year
> I went out into the arena of brush and ink.
> Those followers of "this culture," Ts'ui and Wei,
> Thought me to be like Pan and Yang.

One feels that he might in old age have looked back to the beginnings of his poetic career, splendid as it was, a little less pompously, especially when those followers of Confucian culture, Ts'ui Shang and Wei Ch'i-hsin left a very small mark in Chinese literature. Yet arrogance was a strand of his character. From these lines it can be gathered that Tu Fu's early efforts were in the descriptive *fu* form[3]—Pan Ku (32–92 A.D.) and Yang Hsiung (53 B.C.–18 A.D.) had been two of its great masters in its greatest period—and that his promise and his knowledge were recognized by literary men to whom his work was shown.

The final lines on his boyhood days are quite revealing.

> My nature was spirited; already I was fond of wine;
> I hated evil and maintained unyielding feelings.
> I abandoned those of my own age,
> And associated always with the old.
> Elated with drinking, I gazed on the Eight Limits,
> While common objects all became vague.

The old man seems to have drawn an authentic sketch of the boy who felt himself "different," older and more mature than his con- temporaries; who was stern and capable of censoriousness; who already showed a tendency to set his gaze upon a world which ought to be as much as on the world that was. To this picture, his other old-age memory of himself at fourteen seems at first sight contradictory.

I remember in my fifteenth year my heart was still childish;
Strong as a brown calf, I ran to and fro.
When pears and dates ripened in the courtyard in the eighth month,
In a single day I could climb the trees a thousand times.

One could read these lines with a pleasant feeling of relief that they dispel the image of Tu Fu never having been a boy. In their context,[4] however, they form part of a lament for the decline of his physical strength. Physical achievement was important to Tu Fu, and in the period of his early manhood this side of his nature was to have play.

II A Young Man's Travels

In his twentieth year (731) Tu Fu began a series of travels which were to occupy the greater part of the next ten years. They fell into two major divisions on either side of his unsuccessful attempt at the capital examination in 736. In the first his direc- tion was southeast ("Wu and Yüeh"), in the second east and northeast ("Ch'i and Chao"). In later times, to speak of "travels in Wu and Yüeh" or "travels in Ch'i and Chao" was consciously to identify oneself with Tu Fu, for in this as in so much else the man and his words had entered into the general currency of the language. These travels are known from his later poetry of remi- niscence, not from the poems he wrote at the time, which were not preserved. To the aging and often sick poet of the later wan- derings, the travels of his early manhood must have seemed in- vested with a contrasting carefree lightness.

Tu Fu's starting point cannot be determined. In two of his late poems[5] he refers to meetings forty years earlier at Hsün-hsia (modern I—shih, Shansi), and these may be dated 730. Both poems imply that the stay in Hsün-hsia was not a pleasant mem- ory, and this gives grounds for the suggestion[6] that it could have

been brought about by a flight from the severe floods of the Lo
and Ch'an rivers in that year. This assumes that he was living in
the environs of Lo-yang. Whatever the fact, no cloud was cast
over the travels to the southeast, when Tu Fu later recalled them.

It was still "the full prosperous time of K'ai-yüan" (K'ai-yüan
was the regnal name given to the first two-thirds of Hsüan-tsung's
reign, 713–741).

> When a small city still held ten thousand families.
> The rice was succulent and the millet white;
> Public and private granaries alike were filled.
> On the Nine Provinces' roads were no marauders;
> Distant travelers cared not for a lucky day to start.[7]

Tu Fu is likely to have made his journey to the southeast by
water, down the Yellow River and the canal and then on across
the Yangtse to "Kiang-nan" (south China).

It is reasonably assumed that he spent the next four years in
the area corresponding to the trans-Yangtse part of the modern
province of Kiangsu and to the northern part of the province of
Chekiang. Since this area contained the capital (modern Nanking) and several of the major cities of the Southern Dynasties,
which had maintained themselves for nearly two centuries in the
period of division before the Sui reunification in 589, it was rich
in historical associations of a fairly recent date, as well as of far
earlier times.

Tu Fu gives no clue to why he undertook these travels. He was
in this case traveling away from the capitals of the day to cities
of now somewhat departed splendor so that it cannot be argued
that he was, as many of his contemporaries might be at this stage
in their careers, seeking to catch the eye of the great and influ-
ential. The few friendships, formed at this time and known from
later mention,[8] were, as was usual with him, deep and lasting, but
not important for his advancement. Two of his relatives are
known to have held office in this area, and some have seen a possible connection in this with Tu Fu's travels.[9] There is, however,
no certainty that they were in their posts at this time. In general,
it is perhaps more likely that he had some assured hospitality
before he set out.

Although the excursions in "Wu and Yüeh" are recorded in a
score of lines in *The Wanderings of My Prime* rather than in

travel diaries of many pages, it may not be too fanciful to compare Tu Fu's four years in the southeast to a young seventeenth-century English writer's travels to Italy. The effects of distance and change of landscape, people, and customs could have been similar in degree. The visits to the sites connected with Ho-lu, king of Wu (514–496 B.C.) and to the temple to Wu T'ai-po (eleventh century B.C., uncle of King Wen who founded the Chou dynasty) at Soochow, the reminders of the warrior-king of Yüeh, Kou-chien (496–465 B.C.) at K'uai-chi (modern Shao-hsing) and of the First Emperor of Ch'in (221–208 B.C.) as he crossed the river Che, no doubt nourished the historical sense in Tu Fu. The lakes and rivers, cliffs and valleys quickened his eye to all landscape through the presentation of new forms. It must also have been of interest to him to see the places and scenes described by poets of the Southern Dynasties.

Perhaps, too, these years in these cities where the titles of the ghosts had been higher than those of the living encouraged that taste for the moss-grown and for antique patina, which also found expression in his poetry.

> The Wangs and Hsiehs' style was remote;
> Ho-lu's grave mound was overgrown.[10]

Finally, there is a chance glimpse from a recollection in a later poem[11] of Tu Fu early pursuing his love of painting which was to produce many notable poems in his collection and to add a new genre to Chinese poetry.[12] In Chiang-ning (part of modern Nanking) he saw in the Wa-kuan monastery (built in 364) a painting of Vimalakīrti by the great fourth-century master, Ku K'ai-chih.

In *The Wanderings of My Prime* he expressed lasting regret that these travels had not taken him even further.

> When I went down to the east from Ku-su Terrace,[13]
> I had already prepared to sail upon the sea.
> To this day I have a lingering regret
> That I was not able to investigate Fu-sang.

These lines reveal a flash of the adventurous spirit of the poet, though whether by "Fu-sang" he positively intended Japan or not is hard to confirm or deny. Such a journey would have been the most hazardous he ever undertook.

At some time in 735 he left "Wu-Yüeh," bearing away affectionate memories that were to last for the rest of his life. At K'uei-chou in 766 he wrote

> A merchant Turk leaving down river for Yang-chou
> Reminds me of climbing Hsi-ling's old post-tower.
> "Enquire for me the price of Huai-nan rice;
> I may on impulse make an excursion to the East."[14]

Though these years are unrepresented[15] in Tu Fu's surviving poems, even the scanty knowledge of them that remains makes it possible to recognize their significant part in the formation of the poet.

It seems to have been a very confident young man who was presented by the prefect of Ching-chao for the examination of 736, and his failure to pass must have been a bitter blow to his self-esteem. "Perversely I failed the examination by the Bureau of Merits"[16] makes it clear that he blamed himself rather than the examiner, but offers no clue to why he failed. Failure where twenty or thirty candidates, perhaps one or two percent of the total entrants, passed, hardly needs explanation.

From his disappointment he turned again to travel. If there were no other source, *The Wanderings of My Prime* could lead to the belief that the travels in Ch'i and Chao (corresponding to modern Shantung and southern Hopei) occupied the whole of the "eight or nine years" until his return to Ch'ang-an. It is clear, however, from surviving poems and other works that at least by 741 the "Ch'i-Chao" period was over. It is probable that Tu Fu's father was an assistant prefect at Yen-chou during these years, and Yen-chou may well have been the starting place and point of return of these travels.

However long or short its duration, this period in Tu Fu's career in which he cultivated the active pursuits of riding and hunting explains important aspects of his poetry. The extreme separation of the man of letters from the life of action, which occurred at both earlier and later periods of Chinese history, clearly did not run in the T'ang dynasty. The influences of the "barbarian" Northern Dynasties of the fourth to the sixth centuries were still potent. There was nothing so very remarkable in his time for Tu Fu to play the dashing horseman. To the later study-bound scholar, these violent activities were strange, and in the twentieth

century the further overlay of socialist feeling against so aristo-
cratic a pursuit as hunting is liable to leave the modern Chinese
critic uncomfortable before this stage in Tu Fu's life.

He himself continued to look back with pride to the days when

> I called the hawk in Black Oak Forest;
> I chased wild beasts on Cloud and Snow Ridge.
> I loosed my flying arrows at the gallop;
> Stretching my arm, I brought down a crane.
> Lord Su rejoiced in his saddle,
> Suddenly to have a Ko Ch'iang for companion.[17]

It was certainly not a time which he in any sense rejected or regarded as a youthful extravagance. The only regret that was
liable to assail him was that with age such delights became impossible.

> Suddenly I think of youthful days,
> When frosty dew froze on the steps and door.
> On a Tatar horse I clasped an ornamented bow;
> My humming string was not loosed in vain.
> My long shaft sped after the cunning hare;
> Its swift feathers fitted to the bow's full moon.
> Mournful, the Song of the White-headed;
> Deserted now, the haunts of the gallants.[18]

This poem was probably written in 766. The next year, the re-
membrance of his youthful prowess led him into a serious fall,
as he describes in the delightfully ironic *I Fell from a Horse When
Drunk and My Friends Came to See Me, Bringing Wine.*

> I was once again His Excellency's guest;
> After the party with drunken song I grasped an iron spear;
> Astride a horse, I suddenly recalled my youth;
> With flying hooves I hurtled down Ch'ü-t'ang's rocks.
> From above the river clouds at White Emperor City gate,
> Crouched flat, I descended eight thousand feet.
> White battlements went lightning fast by the purple bridle;
> Eastward, I gained the level ridge from out sky-high walls.
> The river village's rustic dwellings struggled into view;
> I lowered my whip, loosed my reins and went along the bank.
> I had always wanted with my white hairs to startle the masses,
> And of course relied on my youthful ability to ride and shoot.
> How could I know, when I'd enough of headlong rushing,

The "bloodsweater" would gallop on, still spurting foam?
A single unforeseen stumble and I was finally hurt:
In life lively feelings often bring one to shame.[19]

The delight in physical achievement, which could be carried, as he himself recognized here, to the point of foolish bravado, needs to receive its proper emphasis. It is of course a very common human foible to derive great satisfaction from a trifling success in an activity that lies at the pole opposite to one's particular achievement. A suspicion perhaps arises that Tu Fu liked to think himself more the man of action than he really was, that he exaggerated his "ability to ride and shoot." Hyperbole is, after all, a feature of his poetic diction. The suspicion has to remain unresolved, but it is undeniable that the imagery of the horse and hawk are recurrent in Tu Fu's poetry. Poems about horses and hawks form a large and important genre in his work, and, though their subjects may be painted horses or hawks, these are invariably treated as if they were living animals.[20]

III   *Uncertain of Purpose*

By early 741 Tu Fu had built a house in Yen-shih hsien, northeast of Lo-yang, beneath the Shou-yang Hills, near where his famous ancestor Tu Yü and his grandfather Tu Shen-yen were buried. The suggestion[21] that his father had died in 740 seems an acute one, for the mourning period of twenty-seven months could reasonably be placed in the years 740–742. In 742 his aunt Madam P'ei died in Lo-yang. Tu Fu went for the funeral and was entrusted with the composition of her tomb inscription, in which he showed his deep gratitude for her early care of him. He seems now to have moved from Yen-shih to Lo-yang, where he spent the next two years, but how he occupied the time is unknown. The number of surviving poems begins slowly to rise in these years after 740, but their assignment to particular years is in most cases rather arbitrary.

The death of his aunt and the probable death of his father during these years gave him a personal sense of the impermanence of human life, a topic long established as a key theme in Chinese poetry. As an example of an expression of this feeling, the short poem *Lung-men* may be cited.

Lung-men makes a cleft across the countryside;
The post-road trees run out from the city wall.
With its august air the imperial abode lies at hand,
While gold and silver Buddhist temples unfold.
As I come and go, the seasons frequently change;
The ways by water and land go on for ever.
Those whom I encounter on the road,
How many times shall I see in my life?[22]

The Lung-men (Dragon Gate) Gorge became famous in Tu Fu's grandfather's day for the Buddhist sculptures cut into its rocks; it lies on the I River, south of Lo-yang. Tu Fu showed some interest—one should not put it more strongly—at this time in the rival faiths to Confucianism. A number of Buddhist friends appear in his poetry, and he shows some knowledge of the foreign religion as well as native Taoism, but there is no sign that it attracted any positive belief from him.

Both Taoism and Buddhism received encouragement and official support during the first half of the T'ang dynasty. In 735 Emperor Hsüan-tsung had produced a commentary to the *Tao-te-ching* and ordered its study in schools. Four other Taoist books, *Chuang-tzu, Lieh-tzu, Wen-tzu,* and *Keng-sang-tzu* were raised to the status of canonical works (*ching*) in 742. In the previous year, the establishment of temples to Lao-tzu, supposed author of the *Tao-te-ching* and founder of Taoism, was decreed for the two capitals and the prefectures of the empire. Lao-tzu under the surname Li had been regarded as a remote ancestor of the imperial family since the time of the first T'ang emperor. Hsüan-tsung also wrote a commentary to the *Diamond Sutra* in 741.

Tu Fu's interest in Taoism, especially in its immortality-seeking aspects, was no doubt strengthened by his meeting with his older contemporary Li Po (701–62) in 744. Li Po and Tu Fu, contrasted in character and in their individual poetic achievement, were for time to come to occupy together the highest niche in the greatest period of Chinese poetry. Their meetings were confined to the two years 744 and 745, but the attraction of Li Po's quite different personality and the affection he aroused in Tu Fu remained and continued to evoke moving poetry (apparently unanswered) until the older poet's death. How and where they first met cannot be determined with certainty; the general view is that they met in Lo-yang. What can be affirmed from two of Tu Fu's later poems of reminiscence is that Li Po and Tu Fu in company with another poet, Kao Shih, who subsequently became a close friend of Tu Fu, in the autumn of 744 made excursions together to historic sites near the cities of Ch'en-liu (modern K'ai-feng, Honan) and Sung-chou (modern Shang-ch'iu, Honan). Kao Shih had been in this "Liang-Sung" area (so called from the names of states of the first millennium B.C.) for some years,[23] whereas Li Po had arrived here in the summer of 744, after his dismissal from the court at Ch'ang-an.[24] Tu Fu's grandfather's second wife née Lu died at Ch'en-liu in this summer and was buried at Yen-shih in the autumn. This event could provide family reasons for Tu Fu's presence in Ch'en-liu. Kao Shih left in the winter for the south, but Li Po and Tu Fu were to be together again the next year.

The poem, which by common consent is the first addressed by Tu Fu to Li Po, seems very much framed to accord with the Taoist preoccupations of its recipient. With Tu Fu such interests were only of a temporary nature.

> For two years I stayed in the Eastern Capital,
> And my experiences made me hate the tricks and cunning.
> A countryman, faced with the smell of meat,
> Always feels he has not enough vegetable foods.
> How can there be no "green essence" rice
> To make my features glad?
> But, alas, I lack the means to buy major herbs,
> So hills and woods are free of my tracks.
> Lord Li was one of the talents of the Golden Gate,
> But has withdrawn to practise secret searches.
> He too is making excursions in Liang and Sung,
> And is hoping to gather the jade flower.[25]

It was perhaps at this time and under Li Po's influence that Tu Fu made a journey, which he recalled in later poems,[26] across the Yellow River to Wang-wu shan (near modern Yang-ch'eng, Shansi) to visit a Taoist master. The visit proved unsuccessful, since the Taoist had died.

In the spring of 745 Tu Fu was again in Yen-chou (now renamed Lu-chün, since 742), where his father had been assistant prefect. The evidence is provided by two poems written for inscription on the house of a hermit named Chang with whom he formed a happy association.

I

Among the spring hills, without a companion, alone I seek you;
With the ding-ding of wood-cutting the hills seem still quieter.
Along the rocky channel's lingering cold, I go over frozen snow.
In the Stone Gate's evening rays I reach the wooded mound.
Uncoveting, by night you know the aura of gold and silver.
Safe from harm, by day you watch the roaming of the deer.
On impulse plunging deep, we lose our way;
In your presence do I drift like an empty boat?

II

This man often welcomes me,
Inviting me for evening delights to stay.
In the clear pool the carp abound;
Through the spring grasses the deer bleat.
Tu's wine, he kindly presses on me;
Chang's pears, we do not seek elsewhere.
To the village ahead the hill track is steep,
But I return drunk with never a care.[27]

From a much later poem[28] to Li Po there is an indication that, if Tu Fu's memory was not at fault, the two poets were once again together in this spring, but there is no poem of the time to confirm it.

Summer found Tu Fu in Lin-tzu (modern Li-ch'eng, Shantung), where Li Chih-fang was acting prefect. According to a late poem, their friendship began in boyhood so that Tu Fu may well have gone to Lin-tzu to see him. Chih-fang's grandfather's brother Li Yung (678–747), who was prefect of Pei-hai (modern I-tu, Shantung) was also at Lin-tzu on a visit. Li Yung was acknowledged by Tu Fu as an early admirer of his writing,[29] and honored by him in one of his "in memoriam" poems, *Eight Laments*.[30] There are two surviving poems by Tu Fu and one by Li Yung, written for parties they attended together at this time, and the "in memoriam" poem remembers Li Yung pronouncing on the literary men of his day. Li Yung was a great literary lion, and it may be imagined that his encouragement and approval were very important to Tu Fu at this stage in his life.

In the autumn he was back again at Lu-chün for more parties

and for his last meetings with Li Po. In a poem of this time he
first shows the remarkably deep feelings which were to characterize everything he afterwards addressed to Li Po.

> Lord Li has beautiful lines
> Which often resemble Yin K'eng's.
> I too am a visitor to the Tung-meng Hills,
> And I love him as though his brother.
> In drunken sleep, in autumn we share a quilt;
> Hand in hand, daily we walk together.[31]

In the last lines of this poem he writes:

> We are not willing to discuss "hairpins and tablets";
> Unworldly are our feelings for the ocean.

He seems still very much under the influence of the vagabond
Li Po, rejecting an official career (of which "hairpins and tablets"
were the insignia) and accepting the life of withdrawal, sym-
bolized by the ocean. In the years ahead, whenever frustration
descended on Tu Fu, as it did very frequently, the desire for
withdrawal and hermitage makes its appearance in his poetry,
but no extensive reading of his work can admit that this is other
than the expression of frustration. At this moment, however, his
emotions were beginning to tend in the opposite direction.

> As autumn comes, we see ourselves still floating thistle-down;
> Not to have found the cinnabar shames one before Ko Hung.
> In deep drinking, wild singing, vainly to pass one's days,
> To be unruly and arrogant, over whom does one triumph?[32]

This other poem to Li Po shows the impatience of a man past
thirty to be on and doing something in the world. From the dozen
or so extant poems which can be dated with certainty pre-746—a
mere handful of what must have been a very much larger number—rather few of the major characteristics of the mature poet
can be illustrated. They are mainly poems written on social occasions, accomplished but not highly self-revealing. These two
poems of 745 to Li Po begin to show something of the later Tu Fu.

Before the autumn was over, the poets had parted for the last
time. Li Po's farewell poem and the poem he sent after Tu Fu
both refer to autumn. No later poem from Li Po to Tu Fu is
known, nor is there any sign of any interest in Tu Fu's doings in
his later poetry, so that a curious situation obtained with the ex-

pression of deep affection and great concern on the one side and on the other only silence.

IV   *Ten Years in Ch'ang-an*

The hint of impatience with the waste of days in the short poem to Li Po is the only clue to why Tu Fu returned in the winter of 745 or early in 746 to the scene of his earlier failure, the capital Ch'ang-an. No other immediate impulse can be adduced from his writings, but since so much of his poetry returns to the topic during these next ten years, it can safely be concluded that he had decided again to seek a government post. He could hardly have suspected in 746 that he would have to go through almost the whole of these years without achieving this object either by examination or on the strength of his literary accomplishments. Now he was no longer a brilliant young man, encouraged and flattered by his elders, but an established poet himself and a friend of several of the leading poets of his time. "Those who accepted me as a friend were all literary leaders," he wrote in *The Wanderings of My Prime.*

An opportunity for a new attempt by the examination route was presented in 747. The emperor ordered a special examination, commanding those who "possessed a single art," that is, were proficient in one of the prescribed Classics ,to come to the capital. None of the candidates, however, passed, because Li Lin-fu, who had controlled the government as virtual dictator since 736, is said to have feared that the actual state of political affairs might leak out and therefore persuaded the emperor not to conduct the special examination in person. He argued that the rusticity of the candidates might defile the emperor. The examination thus took place under Li Lin-fu's control, and he was able to send a memorial of congratulation to the emperor that there were "no worthy men in the countryside who had been overlooked." These maneuvers are known from the description by another well-known unsuccessful candidate Yüan Chieh (723–72).

Tu Fu expressed his own disappointment in *Twenty-two Rhymes to His Excellency Left Secretary Wei:*

> After the emperor's recent summons,
> I suddenly thought to "seek to stretch myself."
> But in the blue sky my wings drooped;
> Checked, I could not swim freely.[33]

This poem, which must date from after Wei Chi's promotion from prefect of Ho-nan to left secretary, a senior position in the Department of State Affairs,[34] the executive branch of the capital bureaucracy, in the fourth month (May), 748, is one of the first of a number of poems that Tu Fu addressed during these years to men of position whom he hoped might exercise influence on his behalf. Wei Chi had in fact taken the initiative in seeking out the poet. In a note to the first of three surviving poems to Wei—this one sent to him as prefect of Ho-nan at Lo-yang—Tu Fu states that he had heard that Wei had inquired for him at Yen-shih.

The relation of the man of letters to the patron whose favor or aid he seeks must in all ages tend to be invidious, and modern egalitarian man is likely to be especially impatient with the historical forms of patronage. Yet in earlier periods when such patronage was commonplace, the requirement to praise and to flatter probably weighed less heavily. What presumably irked Tu Fu was not so much his need to make such applications for others' aid but their continual failure to bring him success. In such requests for aid the praise he bestows upon the addressees is usually lavish to the point of hyperbole, but the exaggeration has to be seen as conventional and as matching the equally conventional depreciation of himself and the probable inflation of his own difficulties.

Throughout these ten years Tu Fu was forced by his repeated failure to gain the office which he sought into an apparently vacillating and ambivalent attitude. Quite naturally, he sought to maintain his self-esteem by representing the alternatives of staying or going away into "retirement" as subject to his own free choice. If one leaves aside the question of whether Tu Fu was psychologically suited to the life of the "withdrawn scholar" —and fairly obviously he was not—the fact remains that for only very brief periods in his life did he escape from dependence upon relatives and friends.

A man of Tu Fu's class without an official salary was inevitably dependent: his only possible source of earned income, though this too might shade into the area of gift, was commissioned literary work, in particular funerary inscriptions or similar commemorative writings (Li Yung apparently made a considerable income from such works). Without an official salary he was virtually by definition "poor." The poverty of Chinese writers out of office tends to be a conventional expression which masks an actuality running from relative ease to extreme hardship. It is difficult from the mere statement of poverty to determine the degree of the poet's want. From the changes in his personal situation in this decade, his marriage[35] and growing family, and some pressure of external events, Tu Fu's position probably tended steadily to worsen, but this cannot be shown with certainty from his poems. In part this is due to the convention of crying poverty and in part also the fact that a fair proportion of the poems which belong to this period cannot be precisely dated. It is probable, however, that a salary became increasingly a necessity for him.

Tu Fu's poems of this period as a whole show that he steadfastly sought some official post by whatever avenue offered; that his repeated assertions that he would give up the quest and become a "retired scholar" were the expression of frustration rather than of serious intent; that he disliked his dependence on the favor of others, but enjoyed the banquets of the rich, the glitter and luxury of the capital. One needs to avoid the temptation of so many modern Chinese writers to make Tu Fu too heroic as a man. To do so is to risk drawing him as a humbug. For Tu Fu, in spite of all the times that the thought of loneliness enters into his poems, was essentially not a solitary man who wrestled with the decisions of his personal morality. He was a man intensely involved in and with society. He spoke continually of action, because he reacted strongly to events and situations. It is the poet and his poetry which are of heroic proportions, not the man. These ten years are revealing of the many-sidedness, not the narrowness of the poet's character. As illustration, the *Twenty-two Rhymes* to Wei Chi may be given in full.

> Those in silk trousers do not starve to death,
> But the scholar's cap often ruins one's life.
> If you, sir, will quietly listen,
> I should like to state my case.
> Formerly, in the time of my youth,
> I was early a candidate in the capital.
> In reading I wore out ten thousand rolls;
> In plying my brush I was as inspired.
> In *fu*, I was thought Yang Hsiung's match;

In *shih*, I was seen as Tzu-chien's kin.[36]
Li Yung sought after my acquaintance;
Wang Han wished to be my neighbor.
I thought myself to be very outstanding;
That I should at once mount the high road,
To bring my ruler above Yao and Shun
And once again make manners pure.
Such thoughts in the end have come to nought,
But my "going singing" is not that of a hermit.[37]
After bestriding a donkey for ten years,
I lodged in the capital's Spring.
In the mornings I knocked on rich men's doors;
In the evenings followed in sleek horses' dust.
With leftover wine and cold roast meat—
Yet everywhere I hid my bitterness.
After the emperor's recent summons,
I suddenly thought to "seek to stretch myself."
But in the blue sky my wings drooped;
Checked, I could not swim freely.
Though much shamed by your generosity,
I am very conscious of your sincerity;
That whenever you are among your colleagues,
You are fond of reciting new happy lines of mine.
I am as glad as Master Kung at my friend's success,
But I find it hard to bear Yüan Hsien's poverty.[38]
How can my heart be discontented?
It is only that my course is wavering.
Now I am about to go east to the sea,
And intend to leave Ch'in in the west.
But still I love the Chung-nan Hills,
And turn my head to the clear Wei's bank.
Always one intends to repay a single meal;
How deeply one feels at parting from a great minister!
When the white gull vanishes into the void,
Ten thousand *li* off, how can it be tamed?

It is not known how Wei Chi responded to this expression of splendid arrogance, irritation, and some apparent gratitude. The practice of "poem-dropping," exemplified here, was to be continued to a variety of recipients, as was the expressed but unfulfilled intention to go away. The knocking on rich men's doors and the following in sleek horses' dust, however, quite often produced poems of a different color. Writing in reminiscence of this time in *The Wanderings of My Prime,* Tu Fu had kinder memories.

> He who approved me as a companion was truly a worthy prince.
> I trailed my gown to places where fine wine was set.

The worthy prince was Li Chin, Price of Ju-yang, the eldest son of the emperor's elder brother, Li Hsien (679–741), who had in 710 yielded to the future Hsüan-tsung his position as heir-apparent. When Li Hsien died, he was accorded the title of Jang-ti ("Abdicating Emperor") and given an imperial tomb. Li Chin was a patron whom Tu Fu held in the highest regard: he too is the subject of the one of the memorial series *Eight Laments.*[39] The prince's death in 750 must have been a loss to him, for he was clearly one of those whose hospitality gave agreeable days to the poet after his return to Ch'ang-an. In a poem of the time, in which he hails the prince as "a model for every gentleman, a heavenly being whose early virtue has been enhanced," he writes:

> The favor of your summons has come frequently;
> To your esteem my strength is hardly equal.
> A parting of the mists, our first-meeting night;
> At height of autumn, the crisp air clear;
> Winejars stood by the distant bank;
> Ducks and geese slept by the set-out lanterns.[40]

As these years continued, Tu Fu became, at least in the self-representation of his poetry, a somewhat querulous guest at the feast. One is tempted, therefore, to place poems which have no clear date and are free of any note of melancholy or irony in the early years of the Ch'ang-an period. This may be a dangerous proceeding, but the following short poem might have been written when he was quite happily "trailing his gown to places where fine wine was set."

> At sunset it is pleasant to slip the boat;
> The light breeze is slow to raise a wave.
> In the bamboos' depths is a place to stay the guest;
> Amid the lotus' purity a time to enjoy the cool.
> The young men mix iced water;
> The girls clean lotus roots.
> A patch of cloud darkens overhead;
> There must be rain to hasten my poem.[41]

With his noble friends and his poet's tongue, Tu Fu need seldom have gone in want for wine and entertainment, but his membership of Ch'ang-an society was bringing him no nearer to a career.

Besides the approach to men of influence, a more direct channel was open to Tu Fu to try for a post on the strength of his literary merits. This was through the Yen-en kuei ("Favor-Inviting Box"), which enabled a man who considered his ability sufficient to submit writings for the emperor's inspection. Tu Fu had recourse to the submission box on three occasions, though there is dispute about the date in one case. Each time he submitted *fu*,[42] the long descriptive verse form, which by the T'ang period was relatively archaic in language and treatment, and generally was employed for grand and solemn topics. Whether the submission of 751, the three *fu* on the Three Great Ceremonies, was actually his first or his second attempt is not of very great moment;[43] it was clearly the great occasion of his public life. The memory of it remained bright until the end of his days, because these *fu* had received the approbation of the emperor for whom he felt a deep reverence.

> I composed *fu* and sent them to the Bright Radiance Palace.
> The Son of Heaven broke off his meal to summon me;
> The high officials met me in their carriages and robes.

So he wrote in *The Wanderings of My Prime*, and in *Doubt Me Not!*

> I remember when I presented the three *fu* at P'eng-lai Palace,
> I was amazed that in one day my reputation became brilliant.[44]

It is perhaps a little sad that these three *fu*, which obviously meant so much to Tu Fu, have attracted little attention in Tu Fu studies; their significance has largely been limited to a biographical fact. But it is hard for ceremonial and commemorative works, even by a Tu Fu, to have enduring literary interest.

In spite of the colorful description of the emperor breaking off his meal, like his sage predecessor of antiquity, to attend to an important affair of state, the submission of the three *fu* did not rapidly achieve Tu Fu's object. He was instructed to "await an edict" in the Chi-hsien Yüan ("The Academy of Assembled Worthies"), a government institution to which eminent literary men were appointed and which was concerned with the editing of canonical and other books. He was subsequently set a special examination, probably in 752.

> The scholars of Assembled Worthies, like a surrounding wall,
> Watched me ply my brush in the hall of the Secretariat.[45]

He was deemed to have passed this special examination, and he was placed on the list of those awaiting appointment. He was still awaiting appointment, when he submitted another *fu*[46] two years later. His disappointment and indignation at not receiving an immediate appointment—his expectations had, no doubt, run high—were as usual grandly expressed in a poem to two members of the Chi-hsien Yüan, with the usual intention to retire.

> Under the illustrious dynasty I grew white-haired;
> When my path failed, I knocked at Heaven's gate.
> My ambition thrust beyond the stars;
> My words stirred the emperor's majesty.
> The Chief Minister wrote the topics;
> The Ministry of Rites examined my discussions.
> Relying on the wind, I left the fish-hawk's path;
> Following the stream, I came to the dragon gate.
> Yet I ended among the water-serpents' throng;
> How could I listen to the swallows' twittering?
> The blue sky was still far removed;
> To transcending flight I could not soar.
> By scholarship it's truly hard to rise,
> But family fame has perhaps been saved.
> In my old hills are many plants for drugs;
> Their scenery recalls the Peach Blossom Spring.
> I am making ready to return to my village banner,
> But long will my thoughts dwell on the palace walls.
> You have exaggeratedly praised me for my three *fu*;
> It is hard to describe the kindness of you two.[47]

In the phrase "my old hills" Tu Fu is most likely referring to Yen-shih, but there is no evidence that he returned there. From a number of poems it appears that in the later years of this period he was living outside and south of the city in or near Tu Village, where he was regarded as a senior member of the clan.

> In Tu Village there were changes among the elders;
> On the outskirts on every side there were aspens.
> I had a seat of honor from the village's respect;
> Daily I was aware of the hurry of life and death.[48]

It seems also that he owned some land there, for in another
poem he writes:

> I have decided in my life not to make demands of Heaven;
> In Tu Village luckily I have mulberry and hemp fields.[49]

In this new home he was by no means in the wilds, though he
may occasionally make it appear so, but near the villas of the
wealthy. The "rustic of Tu-ling" was still part of Ch'ang-an
literary society.

The surviving pre-746 poems show almost no interest on
Tu Fu's part in the wider world outside his own affairs. When
late in life he remembered the excursions in "Liang and Sung"
with Kao Shih and Li Po, he wrote in the manner of his later self:

> At this time the granaries were full;
> In every direction the empire unfolded.
> The bold man thought of destroying Tatars;
> The general aspired to the chief ministries;
> No princedom was denied to him,
> As he took advantage of his heroic qualities.
> Yu and Yen were piled with munitions of war;
> Their supply was truly burdensome.
> From Wu-men grain and silk were carried
> Over the sea to P'eng-lai.
> Three hundred thousand had to be fed;
> The hunters stirred up the yellow dust.[50]

In 744 there is no evidence of this sort of appreciation of the
burdens of supplying An Lu-shan's huge army in the northeast.

In very many of his poems from the 746–755 period also Tu Fu
seems very preoccupied with his own concerns, above all his
unsuccessful pursuit of a post. It is true that in the *Twenty-two
Rhymes* to Wei Chi he had written of the disappointment of his
hope "to bring my ruler above Yao and Shun," but in context this
hope is fairly selfishly expressed. Yet as he lived in the capital in
the society of those involved more or less intimately with politics
and government, the looming dangers of the current situation
must have been communicated to him. It seems a mistake to
make Tu Fu particularly prescient. Indeed, it may be less erro-
neous to see him as rather slow to realize the political decline of
the later part of Hsüan-tsung's reign. The hardships caused by
the continual border wars, however, began to be impressed on

him, as the tide of battle turned against the Chinese armies. The defeat of Governor-General Kao Hsien-chih by the Abbāsid Arab troops at the Talas River in 751 in fact marked the beginning of the end of T'ang power in central Asia.

Song of the War Carts of about 750 is one of the earliest examples of the adaptation of the popular ballad style, which Tu Fu was to exploit with such distinctive effect.[51] Together with the first series entitled *Going Out of the Frontiers*, it shows the emergence in Tu Fu's poetry of those qualities of human sympathy and of consciousness of the distress of war, which have received especial acclaim, most of all in twentieth-century China.

Song of the War Carts

Carts creak, horses neigh;
Marching men with bows and arrows at each waist.
Parents, wives and children run to see them off;
The dust obscures Hsien-yang Bridge.
They clutch at clothes, stumble, block the road, weep;
The sound of their weeping goes straight up to meet the clouds.

If a passer-by questions the marching men,
The marching men merely say: "Conscripted, we hurry.
Some, since fifteen, in the north guarded the Ho;
Now, at forty, in the west we stand garrison.
In the past the village heads gave us manhood turbans;
Returned with heads white, we go back to the frontiers.
At the frontiers our streaming blood has formed a sea,
But our martial emperor's thoughts of conquest are not ended.
Sir, have you not heard
How two hundred of our prefectures east of the Mountains,
A thousand villages, ten thousand hamlets, grow brambles?
Even where strong women grasp the hoe and plough,
And corn grows, the dikes and fields are unrecognizable.
Moreover, though Ch'in soldiers can endure bitter fighting,
They are driven on like dogs and fowls.

Sir, though you have enquired,
Dare soldiers air their grievances?
As for the present winter,
They have not yet released the Kuan-hsi troops,
But the district officials relentlessly seek taxes.
Where are the taxes to come from?
We truly know the evil of raising sons;

Opposite are the joys of raising daughters.
If you have a daughter, you may still marry her to a neighbor;
If you have a son, buried, he will lie with the weeds.
Sir, have you not seen, near Kokonor,
The white bones from olden times, no one collects?
New ghosts complain, old ghosts lament;
At night or in the rain their voices moan.[52]

The sudden appearance of *Song of the War Carts,* with its simple language and loose form among the social verse and the elaborately modulated and grandiloquent poems to patrons, comes as a surprise. It had in fact its literary ancestors, and his friend Li Po was also drawing on the same sources for similar themes at this time.[53] But Tu Fu's new ballads are truly individual and show a greater degree of difference than do Li Po's from the rest of his poetry of the same time. The reader is faced at this point with the first important indications of the possible extent of his range. It is tempting to try to find psychological answers for the widening of Tu Fu's awareness and the deepening of his sympathy, to see this as arising out of his own increasing personal difficulties and disappointments. Yet it seems doubtful that if all the poems of this period could be accurately dated and very much more were known of the details of his life, a neat and satisfying explanation would result. In these last of his formative years the final complex features of a great poet were taking shape.

In a poem written at the time of the Double Third Festival, perhaps of 753, he employed the ballad form he used for the *Song of the War Carts* in a different manner. The language of *Song of Fair Women* can hardly be called simple, although the exotic nature of its subject matter inevitably imposes its particular requirement. This poem has been universally seen by critics as a thinly veiled attack on the luxury and viciousness of the Yang family. Yang T'ai-chen, known in popular history as Yang Kuei-fei, had become Emperor Hsüan-tsung's chief concubine (*kuei-fei*) in 745. At the same time her three elder sisters were given mansions in the capital, and in 748 they were given noble titles, as Lady of Han, Lady of Kuo, and Lady of Ch'in. Her cousin Yang Kuo-chung was also an intimate of the emperor and was given increasingly important government posts until on the death of Li Lin-fu at the beginning of 753 he was appointed chief minister.

On the third day of the third month the air is fresh;
By the bank of Ch'ang-an's stream there are many fair women;
With splendid bearing and remote manner, pure and true;
Their skins delicate and smooth, bones and flesh in true balance.
Their embroidered silk garments shine in the late spring sun,
Worked with golden peacocks or silver unicorns.
On their heads what have they?
Hair-ornaments with glittering kingfishers hanging by their
  temples.
On their backs what can be seen?
Pearl-studded stomachers closely fitting their bodies.
Among them in the cloud-painted tents, the relatives of the
  Pepper Room,
On whom have been bestowed the titles of Great Kuo and Ch'in.
Red camel hump is served out of a green cauldron;
On crystal plates is brought in white fish.
The rhinoceros-horn chopsticks, through satiety, long are unused;
Morsels, fine-shredded by the phoenix knife, lie vainly heaped.
Palace attendants come with flying reins, not stirring dust;
From the imperial kitchens continuously bringing the Eight
  Delicacies.
Pipes and drums sadly sound, moving ghosts and spirits;
Guests and retainers abound, proving the host's high station.
Late he comes on horseback, how slowly!
At the pavilion dismounts, sinks upon the embroidered cushions.
Willow catkins, falling snowlike, cover the white duckweed;
A green bird flies away with a red napkin in its mouth.
"Warm your hand and you may be burnt": his power is beyond
  compare.
Take care not to approach the Chief Minister's anger![54]

An edge of irony has certainly been given to this poem, but the
poet's delight in the magnificence of the scene which he was describing cannot be denied. If the criticism of luxury is here not so
direct as it became in later poems, it may be also that the evils of
luxury and the burden it imposed on the common people were
not yet so strongly felt by Tu Fu. He was still hoping for a post,
and in the memorial with which he presented the *fu,* submitted
in 754, he was prepared to refer to Yang Kuo-chung in what was,
in the light of history, a distressingly fulsome manner.[55]

The autumn of 754 was difficult in Ch'ang-an, for the rains
continued for more than sixty days without stopping. The walls
of houses collapsed, the harvest was ruined and prices rose; ra-

tions of rice at fixed prices had to be issued from the government granaries to prevent starvation. Rain, since it forms the subject of no less than fifty poems in Tu Fu's whole collection, must be considered a significant topic in his poetry. The three-poem series *Sighing over the Autumn Rains* may be given as an early example. It also shows the degree of his concern over what was a matter of widespread hardship.

I

In the rains all the plants autumn-wither and die;
Yet below the steps the "eyebright's" blooms are fresh.
Its leaves, put forth, fill its stems with a kingfisher feather canopy;
Its opened flowers are countless golden coins.
The cold wind sighs and blows keenly on you;
I fear you will after find it hard to stand alone.
Up in the hall the scholar, vainly becoming white-headed,
Facing the wind, thrice breathes your fragrant tears.

II

With unseasonal storms and rain autumn is confused;
The Four Seas and the Eight Wilds share a single cloud.
A horse going and an ox coming can no more be distinguished;
How should the muddy Ching and the clear Wei be separated?
The grain heads grow ears, the millet panicles are black;
Yet no report comes from the farmers and peasants.
In the city for a peck of rice one gives one's bedding;
Only let the bargain be made, what matter if it's fair!

III

Whose lot is as bad as the plain-robed man of Ch'ang-an's?
Locked up within his rustic door, keeping his narrow walls.
The old man does not go out into the tall jungle,
Though the children without a care run in wind and rain.
The rain's sound, whistling, hastens on the early cold;
The Tatar goose's wings are damp; it can hardly fly high.
Since autumn came, we have not seen the daylight;
From mud and puddles when will the earth be dry?[56]

These are justly admired poems, for they exhibit a freely flowing blend of literary reminiscence with the description of actuality, of "poetic" effects of flowers blooming in the rain with simple touches of his children running about regardless of the storms. Yet the stance is self-centered ("Whose lot is as bad?") and not modified, as it would generally have been in his later poetry, by a direct expression of solicitude for the probably greater sufferings of others. In fairness, attention needs to be drawn to another poem of this autumn, one written for the Double Ninth Festival and addressed to his friend Ts'en Shen.[57] Here he does think of the disaster of the rains for the common people.

> Oh! Alas for the common folk!
> Their harvest cannot be saved.

The difficulties of this autumn reduced Tu Fu to the point of desperation where he decided to move his family away from Ch'ang-an to Feng-hsien (modern P'u-ch'eng, Shensi), about eighty miles northeast of Ch'ang-an. The magistrate of Feng-hsien was like Tu Fu's wife surnamed Yang so that it is possible that he was related. A maternal relative of Tu Fu (a Ts'ui) had a post in nearby Po-shui. The removal must certainly have been prompted by the hope of some more adequate support for his family than he was able to secure at Ch'ang-an. At Feng-hsien was the tomb of Hsüan-tsung's father, Jui-tsung, who had abdicated in favor of his son after a short reign of two years in 712. Tu Fu ends a long poem describing the mausoleum and its environs and the local officials with a picture of his arrival at Feng-hsien.

> Unlucky, I have left lower Tu;
> A wanderer, I have crossed the muddy Ching.
> In a scholar's shabby short coat,
> Drifting, a floating duckweed.
> In a famine year my children grow thin;
> On the evening road my tears fall.
> Our host has pity on an old horse;
> The yamen admits autumn fireflies.
> The life of a wanderer can't be happy;
> From the stupor of utter grief he doesn't awake.
> How may I shake off the world's bonds
> And range at large over the blue ocean?[58]

After he had settled his family in Feng-hsien, he seems to have spent the winter there, but by the spring of 755 he was back in the capital. In spite of some appreciation of growing dangers, apparent in his poetry of the last years, he could not know that this year was to be one of the most memorable dates in Chinese history. The rebellion which An Lu-shan launched in December,

755, was to bring this middle-aged man to moments of great intensity of feeling which called forth his greatest poetry. The effect of the rebellion was to raise Tu Fu from the ranks of major poets and give him claim to the title of greatest. For at the end of 755, as he came by Chinese reckoning to his 45th year, the poems which it would be impossible to exclude from any general anthology of Chinese poetry still remained to be written. On the eve of the rebellion he had completed almost ten long and frustrating years in Ch'ang-an.

The first part of the long poem *Five Hundred Words to Express My Feelings When I Went from the Capital to Feng-hsien,* written at the end of 755 apparently before the news of the rebellion reached him, forms a kind of *apologia* for his efforts to gain a post through all these years, efforts that he himself deemed worthy of ridicule. His excuse is that he cannot change his nature and so cannot rid himself of his ambition.

> From Tu-ling a plain-robed man,
> Aging, his desires yet stupider;
> To offer himself, oh how foolish!
> Daring to emulate Chi and Ch'i.
> He just achieves no purpose;
> His white head but bears hardship.
> Only when his coffin closes will it end,
> For after this ambition he ever hankers.
> The whole year, anxious for the masses,
> He sighs and his heart within him burns;
> Laughed at by his old school-fellows,
> He raises his song ever more ardently.
> Not that he has no desire for rivers and seas,
> There, free of care, to spend the days and months,
> But he lives in the time of a Yao and Shun ruler,
> Of whom he cannot bear to take leave for ever.
> Already there are materials for galleries and temples;
> Surely means are not lacking to roof the hall?
> The sunflower turns towards the sun:
> Things' nature truly cannot be taken away.
> And he considers the ants,
> How they only seek their own holes.
> Why should they emulate the great whale
> And strive like it to lie on the vast ocean?
> From this he is aware of life's workings;
> Only he is ashamed of "paying calls."

> He has struggled on until the present;
> Is he willing to end in the dust?
> After all he is shamed by Ch'ao and Yu,
> Who could never change their principles.
> By deep drinking for a while he comforts himself;
> Breaking into song, he largely puts an end to grief.[59]

The grand note of the *Twenty-two Rhymes* to Wei Chi is still there: he is still willing in his view of his possible service to the emperor to compare himself with Chi and Ch'i, worthy ministers of the legendary golden age of Yao and Shun. Yet he is a little sadder and wiser. He is prepared on one hand to admit the court might have ministers enough ("Already there are materials for galleries and temples...."), and on the other seems ready to recognize the need for some compromise in political life and so is ashamed before Ch'ao-fu and Hsü Yu, two types of the incorruptible hermit.

Although he still refers to himself in this poem as a "plain-robed man," a man without office, Tu Fu had at long last been given an official post. He was appointed police commissioner for the district of Ho-hsi, some fifty miles northeast of Feng-hsien, where his family was staying. This was a common first official appointment, but one where he would have found the duties unpleasant. His friend Kao Shih had occupied a police commissionership and had complained of the distressing task of inflicting beatings on the common people. When Kao Shih quit this post for a secretaryship on the staff of Ko-shu Han, governor-general of the frontier region of Wu-wei, Tu Fu in his farewell poem wrote:

> He has escaped from his police commissionership,
> And for the first time got away from the beating rods.[60]

So not surprisingly Tu Fu declined the appointment. He was then given a new appointment as adjutant in the Office of the Right Commander of the Heir-Apparent's Palace Guard. He celebrated the event with *Humorous Offering After the Post was Settled.*

> I am not to be Police Commissioner at Ho-hsi;
> I should have been sorry for that "to bend my back."
> An old fellow, I am afraid of bustle;
> In the Guard Commander's office I can go leisurely.
> My deep drinking requires a small salary;

My wild singing has the protection of the court.
My ideas of returning to my old hills are ended;
I turn and face the wind's whirling.[61]

The descent from seeking office in order to become a great
minister of a sage emperor to welcoming a small salary to satisfy
his drinking needs is indeed in the best tradition of the Chinese
poet's self-mockery. Tu Fu's jesting poem presumably hid both
disappointment and relief at obtaining some salary. Had he been
extraordinarily unlucky to wait so long? It is easy out of sympathy
with the poet to form a perhaps exaggerated idea of a conspiracy
to keep him out and to see the final granting of this unimportant
post as an attempt to keep him quiet. Negatively, it may be possible to say that if Tu Fu had been of an easier nature, he might
have secured appointment in the earlier years of the Ch'ang-an
period, since his cousin Tu Wei, who appears several times in
his poems, was son-in-law to Li Lin-fu.

If one compares him with his friends of the time, his lot was
not exceptionally hard. The two comparative "successes," Su Yü
(Tu Fu's hunting companion of the Ch'i-Chao period), who
became vice-rector of the Imperial University in 754, and Cheng
Ch'ien, who was given a special academic appointment as professor of the College for the Extension of Literature in 750, were
probably both older men. Cheng Ch'ien, in particular was a
scholar of very wide range, as well as being an outstanding
painter and calligrapher. Kao Shih and Ts'en Shen, the former
five to ten years older than Tu Fu, the latter three years younger,
were not notably more successful than he was. Kao Shih, after
passing a special examination in 749, was given a police commissionership, which after two or three years he resigned out of dislike of its duties. He then took a private appointment on the staff
of Governor-General Ko-shu Han in 753. Ts'en Shen passed second on the list of the regular examination of 744 and received an
appointment similar to that Tu Fu accepted in 755. Subsequently
he left the capital for secretaryships to frontier governors-general
of the same kind as Kao Shih's. There are in fact indications that
Tu Fu contemplated the same step.

There is a general presumption that Tu Fu's appointment came
late in 755, not long before the visit to his family, described in
the famous *Five Hundred Words*. He had perhaps not even entered on his duties and for this reason still felt himself a "plain-

robed" man. Perhaps he now hoped to make some better provision for his family. Tu Fu, in separation from his family, wrote poems of the deepest affection for his wife and his children. *In the Moonlight on the Hundred and Fifth Night,* which may well have been written on April 1, 755, could be the earliest example.

> I have no family on Cold Food eve,
> But I have tears like silver waves.
> Since there is one who chops the moon's cassia,
> Its clear light ought to be yet brighter.
> In separation she puts off her red flowers;
> I imagine how she wrinkles her dark brows.
> The Herdboy and the Maid idly have sad thoughts;
> In autumn time they still will cross the River.[62]

The hope that Tu Fu and his wife, like the star-lovers, would be together in autumn was fulfilled, since there is a poem for the Double Ninth,[63] which must be for the festival of 755, and which would place him in Feng-hsien on October 18. His return from Feng-hsien to Ch'ang-an, his appointment and return once again to Feng-hsien have thus to be fitted into a period of about two months.

When he reached Feng-hsien for the second time, with the glad news of his appointment, tragedy awaited him. In his brief absence he had lost a baby son, by his own statement from hunger. He describes his feelings in the concluding lines of the *Five Hundred Words.*

> My dear wife had gone to a different district;
> Our "ten mouths" were divided by wind and snow.
> How could I for long not care for them?
> So I must go and share their hunger and thirst.
> When I entered the gate, I heard wailing:
> My little son had died of hunger.
> Why should I forbear to lament?
> The village lane indeed sounds with sobs.
> What shames me is to be his father,
> When lack of food has brought his early death.
> How was I to know, when the harvest was excellent,
> That poverty would have such urgency?
> All my life I have been free of taxes;
> My name was not enrolled for military service.
> If the path I tread is yet bitter,

The common man must truly be troubled.
Silently I think of men who have lost their land,
And thence remember the soldiers on distant frontier guard.
My anxiety rises as high as the Southern Hills,
Boundless and not to be controlled.

This ending is characteristically "Tu Fu" or, in other words, is fully typical of his mature style. This hundred-line poem—and such sustained efforts are comparatively rare in Chinese *shih*-poetry—stands at the point of transition to what have been called in this study "the essential years," the years which embrace most of the "anthology" poems and in which Tu Fu may be regarded as reaching his greatest heights.

CHAPTER 2

The Essential Years

FIVE HUNDRED *Words to Express My Feelings When I Went from the Capital to Feng-hsien* gives no indication whatever that the great rebellion which was to draw a sharp line down the middle of the T'ang period had started. Had the news already reached Tu Fu, it would have been impossible for him to have kept it out of the poem. The second section of the poem in which he starts to describe his journey, therefore, has an air of foreboding with something of the quality of Byron's "There was a sound of revelry by night." For on his way to Feng-hsien, Tu Fu had to pass by the Li-shan on which was the Hua-ch'ing Palace with its hot spring. Here in his favorite winter resort the emperor was installed with the Lady Yang and the court, and here he was to receive news of the rebellion. Tu Fu's criticism of the luxury of the court is this time direct and biting. The couplet beginning "Inside the red gates ..." has been endlessly quoted.

> At the year's end every plant has fallen;
> By the rushing wind the high ridges are rent.
> In the imperial thoroughfare the cold is intense,
> As the traveler sets out in the middle of the night.
> In the frost's sharpness my belt snaps;
> My fingers are too stiff to join it.
> By early morning I have passed the Li-shan,
> On whose height the imperial couch is set.
> Ch'ih-yu banners fill up the cold sky;
> From marching feet cliff and valley are smooth.
> Above the Jasper Pool there is a thick mist;
> The Imperial Guards touch each other's lances.
> Our ruler's ministers are detained in pleasure;
> The music starts and rolls away into the distance.
> Those permitted to bathe are all "long cap-strings";
> To share in the feast is not for "short coarse gowns."
> The silk distributed in the vermilion court

Came originally from poor women.
Whips lashed their husbands
To gather the levies for the capital.
Our sage with his ample generosity
Truly desires his country's prosperity.
If his ministers neglect the supreme principles,
Our ruler surely does not disregard such things!
Many gentlemen fill the court,
And the good among them must tremble.
Still more when they hear the palace plate
Is all in the houses of the Wei and Ho.
In the central hall immortals dance;
Their fair forms cast a silken mist.
The guests are warmed with sable furs,
While sad pipes follow shrill citherns.
The guests are urged to camel-pad soup,
To frosted oranges and fragrant tangerines.
Inside the red gates wine and meat go bad;
On the roads are bones of men who died of cold.
Splendor and decay are but a foot apart;
The sadness is not to be twice told.[1]

Reading this, one has the feeling that Tu Fu had indeed caught the sounds of imminent disaster and had become more certain in his own attitudes.

The An-Shih rebellion, as it is commonly called in Chinese sources from the names of An Lu-shan and his principal lieutenant Shih Ssu-ming, was an example of the "border-general disaster," of allowing military power to become concentrated in the hands of a commander who by creating a more or less permanent military organization could establish his independence of central control. The policy of Li Lin-fu in the latter part of Hsüan-tsung's reign of creating frontier military command areas under governors-general who had been successful soldiers in the frontier wars prepared the typically dangerous situation. The non-Chinese origins of these governors-general (and of many of their subordinate officers) could seem to have heightened the risk. In fact, of the foreign governors-general, while An Lu-shan revolted, the others remained loyal to the dynasty, and An Lu-shan was encouraged and aided by the support of dissident "pure" Chinese clans of Northeastern China.[2]

An Lu-shan had been preparing his position over a long period.

He was first appointed governor-general of P'ing-lu, the north-eastern border command in 742; the adjacent northern command was given to him in 744; the area of Ho-tung was added to his combined command in 751. Now in the eleventh month (December), 755, he moved south from his base at Fan-yang (near modern Peking) with the professed object of removing Yang Kuo-chung. The prefectures of Ho-pei Province (corresponding roughly to the modern province of the same name) fell to him without resistance and he advanced on the eastern capital, Lo-yang. In a little more than a month from his setting out Lo-yang was in his hands, and the hastily assembled imperial forces were falling back on the T'ung-kuan, the pass where the road to Ch'ang-an could be barred. Fortunately for the loyalist forces An Lu-shan did not press on firmly against Ch'ang-an but busied himself with the creation of a new dynasty. He declared himself emperor of Great Yen on the first day of the new Chinese year (February 5, 756).

The general view of the chronologists is that Tu Fu returned from Feng-hsien to the capital at the beginning of 756, and one might expect him to have done so. There is, however, no evidence for this, unless one accepts the doubtful assignment of one or two poems to this time. If he did make the journey, by the summer he was back in Feng-hsien and paying a visit to his Ts'ui maternal relative, who was police commissioner at Po-shui. The second half of a poem he wrote on this occasion gives what was probably the general expectation of the moment, that the war should soon be over.

> As we sit a long while, the wind becomes stronger;
> When evening comes, the hills turn bluer;
> Facing us is a hundred-foot-long dragon,
> Bursting forth into cleaving whirlpools.
> Whence comes the thunder in the empty air?
> It is its rumbling through the earth's veins.
> Miasmic vapors tower up in a haze;
> Water-sprites numerously moan.
> K'un-lun and K'ung-t'ung peaks,
> We turn and see as undivided.
> On the front veranda sink the reflected rays;
> In its sheer solitude Hua Peak reddens.
> The aura of war spreads over wood and hill;

The gleam of rivers mingles with lance and arrow.
I know they are the minister's troops;
His "iron" cavalry mass like clouds and mist.
Jade cups now are insipid and tasteless,
But the Tatars are surely not powerful foes.
My drawn-out song makes the rafters shake;
My tears stream down upon my gown and mat.
Man's life is half sorrow, half joy;
In the world there's good fortune and ill.
I am sad for those soldiers from a myriad lands,
Who for a noble ruler prepare to chastise the barbarian.
Fierce generals are deployed in numbers;
Imperial counselors devise excellent plans.
When will the Eastern City be freed?
The soldiers still are not sent home.
I have to break off this fine feast;
It is hard to withstand the pressing of time.
Three times I sigh by the food and wine:
How shall things be as once they were?[3]

Things were not to be as once they were. Soon after the time that this poem was written, the "minister," Kao Shih's general, Ko-shu Han, as a result of repeated urgings from the court, led his troops from their fortress position at T'ung-kuan and was utterly routed. The way to Ch'ang-an was open and the emperor fled.

With the emperor went the Lady Yang, her three sisters, the heir-aparent and other members of the imperial family, Yang Kuo-chung and other ministers, under the protection of palace-guard troops. They set out for Ch'eng-tu in the southwest, and on the second day out at Ma-wei post-station came the tragic end to the emperor's great romance. The troops killed Yang Kuo-chung, on suspicion of treason, and with him his son and his cousins, the Lady of Han and the Lady of Ch'in (Lady Yang's other sister escaped only to be killed soon after). The emperor was then forced to allow his favorite concubine to be put to death. At Ma-wei too, the heir-apparent, Li Heng, was persuaded to leave his father, and he went north to create a rallying point for loyalist forces, while Hsüan-tsung went on to Ch'eng-tu. Before the old emperor reached there, Li Heng (known to history by his posthumous name of Su-tsung) had been proclaimed emperor at Ling-wu (in modern Kansu).

With the collapse of the T'ung-kuan defenses and the fall of the capital, Tu Fu felt it necessary to flee from Feng-hsien, and he took his family north to the prefecture of Fu-chou, where he settled them in a place called Ch'iang Village. A year later, he recalled the experience in *P'eng-ya Road.*[4]

> I remember, when first we fled from the rebels,
> We went north through dangers and difficulties.
> In the depths of the night on the P'eng-ya road
> The moon shone over the Po-shui Hills.
> My whole family traveled long on foot;
> Whenever we met anyone, we were very ashamed.
> Now and then, in the valleys birds sang,
> But we saw no wanderers returning.
> My silly daughter in her hunger bit me;
> I feared tigers and wolves would hear her cries.
> To my bosom I pressed tight her mouth,
> But she struggled and cried the louder.
> My little boy pretended to be understanding,
> But always looked for bitter plums to eat.
> In ten days on half there were thunderstorms;
> Through the mud we struggled to lead each other on.
> We had no provision against the rain;
> The path was slippery and our clothes cold.
> Sometimes, after great hardships,
> In a whole day we made only a few miles.
> Wild fruits supplied our food;
> Low branches became our house-beams.
> Mornings, we walked in water, flowing over rocks;
> Evenings, we lodged among mists at the sky's edge.

Leaving his family in Ch'iang Village, Tu Fu presumably attempted to join the new emperor at Ling-wu, but his next poems show him to be in Ch'ang-an so that it is concluded that he had been captured and taken there by a band of the rebels. Since captive officials were generally sent by the rebels to Lo-yang, Tu Fu does not seem to have been regarded as a very valuable prize, for he seems to have been left in Ch'ang-an under no particular restraint. In the eight months or so of his enforced stay in Ch'ang-an he wrote the most beautiful and most moving of all his poems. The earliest perhaps, since it contains suggestions of autumn, was *Moonlit Night,*[5] one of the finest love poems in a literature, not noted for this genre, which was written in longing for his wife.

Tonight the Fu-chou moon,
In her chamber alone she watches.
From afar I pity my little children
Who know not enough to remember Ch'ang-an.
With fragrant mist her cloud-hair-knots are damp;
In the chill moonlight her jade arms are cold.
When shall we lie within the empty curtains
And it shine on both, our tear-traces dry?

Here Tu Fu used the *lü-shih* form with its tonal prescription and
its parallelism[6] with a skill which prevented the art detracting
anything from the sincerity of the emotion. In *Lament for a
Prince* he used the ballad meter of *Song of the War Carts* in
sympathy for a less humble being, fallen on adversity. The pre-
cipitate flight of Hsüan-tsung had left to their fate those imperial
relatives not living within the inner palace-city. The close references to the current situation show Tu Fu to be making his poetry
out of immediate history, as he was to continue to do through the
long years of rebellion.

A white-headed crow from Ch'ang-an's city wall,
Flying by night, croaked over Staying-Autumn Gate,
And going to men's houses, pecked at the mansions,
Whence great officials fled to escape the Tatars.
The golden whip was broken, the nine-horse team died;
The family did not wait to gallop away together.
At his waist a precious girdle of pink coral,
The pitiable prince weeps by the roadside.
When I ask him, he will not tell his name,
But says he would from wretchedness beg to be a slave.
A hundred days he has skulked among the thorns;
On his body nowhere is there whole skin.
The founder's descendants all have prominent noses;
The dragon seed is naturally unlike ordinary men.
"The wolf is in the city, the dragon is in the wild.
Prince, carefully protect your precious person!
I dare not talk long with you on a main highway.
And may stay for you only for a moment.
Last night the east wind blew the stench of blood,
And from the east came camels to fill the old capital.
The stout lads of Shuo-fang, strong and skillful;
Once how brave and keen, now become how clumsy!
I have heard that the emperor has abdicated his throne;
That the imperial power in the north subdues the Uighur chief;

And men of Hua-men slash their faces and beg leave to wipe away the
    shame.
Take care not to say a word! Others are spies!
Oh! my prince, be not careless!
From the Five Tombs the auspicious aura is never absent!"[7]

In spite of his finally encouraging words to the prince (and to
himself) that the spirit of the T'ang house was still potent, Tu Fu
was to have to record more disasters in his poetic history before
the year was out. Early in the tenth month Emperor Su-tsung
had moved from Ling-wu to a new position nearer to Ch'ang-an
at P'eng-yüan (modern Ning-hsien, Kansu). Fang Kuan, who had
been a vice-minister in the former government and who was later
to play an important part in Tu Fu's personal history, now re-
quested that he might lead troops to recover the capital. Su-tsung
gave his permission. Fang divided his forces into three groups
and generally (he was no soldier) followed archaic tactics, de-
rived from his classical studies. Two of his groups engaged the
rebels at Ch'en-t'ao, west of Ch'ang-an on the twenty-first day of
the tenth month (November 17) and lost forty thousand men. In
the capital, Tu Fu recorded the disaster in *Lament for Ch'en-t'ao*.[8]

> In winter's first month from good families in ten prefectures
> The sons' blood became the water in the Ch'en-t'ao marsh.
> The countryside is deserted, the sky clear, no sound of battle,
> For forty thousand loyal troops have died on the same day.
> The Tatar horde returns with blood-washed arrows,
> Still singing Tatar songs, to drink in our marketplace.
> The citizens turn their heads and cry out to the north;
> Day and night they still yearn for the imperial army to come.

A second battle followed two days later at a place called Ch'ing-
fan and again Fang Kuan was defeated. After this second defeat
Tu Fu was anxious to urge caution upon the loyalist commanders.

> *Lament for Ch'ing-fan*
> Our army at Ch'ing-fan camped by the eastern gate;
> In winter they watered their horses at T'ai-po Hills.
> The "Yellow-heads" and the Hsi daily advanced west;
> Some of their horsemen with bent bows made raids.
> The mountains are snowy, the rivers ice, the country is bare;
> Black is the beacons' smoke, white are men's bones.
> How may I send a letter to our armies:
> Bear to wait for next year and be not hasty![9]

As this disastrous year of 756 approached its end, Tu Fu in the midst of the rebels in Ch'ang-an could do nothing except write poetry. But his lines, still very personal in their statement, could be a symbol of the distress of a nation.

> On the battlefield wailing are many new ghosts;
> In his grief reciting, a lonely old man.
> Tumbled clouds hang down in the twilight;
> Driving snow dances in the whirling wind.
> The ladle is put by; in the jar is no green.
> The stove is still there; the fire but seems red.
> From many prefectures all news is cut off;
> In grief I sit and just write in the air.
>
> *Facing the Snow*

News, carried by unknown hands, did reach Tu Fu. He had a letter which told him that his brothers were safe, though far away in the east, and he heard that his sister had married (and was perhaps already widowed) and was also far away in Chung-li (modern Feng-yang, Anhwei). He apparently received fairly up-to-date reports of the fighting, as in January 757 he was writing a poem of urgent military advice, *Block the Lu-tzu Pass!*[10] The Lu-tzu Pass (not far from Yen-an, famous in twentieth-century Chinese history) was the gateway from the north into the areas west of the Yellow River. With T'ai-yüan invested by a huge rebel army, Tu Fu feared a drive upon Su-tsung's headquarters at P'eng-yüan.

The coming of spring in the captured city seemed to Tu Fu astonishingly inappropriate and provided him with the ironic contrasts of his most famous short poem.

> The country is destroyed but hills and rivers remain;
> In the city, spring, with plants and trees thick.
> In sorrow at the time, the flowers are splashed with tears;
> In grief at separation, the birds alarm the heart.
> Beacon fires have linked three months;
> Family letters are worth ten thousand pieces.
> My white hair, through scratching, is still shorter;
> It very nearly fails to support my hairpin.
>
> *Spring Yearning*[12]

This, like *Facing the Snow*, can be read as a personal poem of personal anguish, but also like the former poem, carries on to universality beyond the limits of one man's grief. This can be emphasized by the comparison of *Remembering My Young Son*,[13] also from this time.

> Chi-tzu is still parted from me in spring.
> While orioles' songs are filling the warm air.
> In my separation I am startled by the season's change;
> His cleverness, with whom should I discuss?
> Where there is a stream by a lonely mountain road,
> A rustic gate in a village of ancient trees,
> I remember him; and in my sorrow simply doze,
> As I warm my back, crouched on the sunny porch.

Here his grief is confined within a personal frame, and there are no ambiguities to extend the feeling beyond it.

The insensate quality of Nature is more directly and sternly rebuked in *Lament by the River*. This poem is the first brief treatment of the theme of the love of Hsüan-tsung and Yang Kuei-fei, which was to continue to attract poets, storytellers, and dramatists down to the present day. The scene is the Curving Stream (*Ch'ü-chiang*), the artificial waterway at the southeastern corner of the city, which had been one of the chief pleasure resorts of Ch'ang-an society.

> I, an old rustic from Shao-ling, weep with stifled sobs;
> On a spring day secretly walking by a bend of the Curving Stream.
> Locked are the thousand gates of the riverside palaces;
> For whom are the slim willows and new rushes green?
> I remember the rainbow banners coming down to the South Park.
> And everything in the Park coming alive with color.
> The First Lady of the Chao-yang Palace
> Rode in one carriage by her lord's side.
> Before it palace women with bows and arrows,
> Their white horses champing on golden bits.
> Bending back to face the sky, one shot at the clouds,
> And with one arrow dropped two birds in flight.
> Bright eyes, white teeth, where are they now?
> The blood-soiled, wandering ghost cannot return.
> The clear Wei River flows east, the Sword Pass is remote;
> From her who has gone to him who stays there are no tidings.
> A man who has feelings must weep upon his breast,
> But you, river waters, river flowers, do you never care?
> In the evening the Tatar cavalry fill the city with dust;
> As I go to the southern city, I gaze longingly to the north.[14]

Toward the end of January 757 An Lu-shan had been murdered in a palace coup in Lo-yang and replaced as rebel emperor by his son An Ch'ing-hsü. The uneasy situation in Lo-yang seems to have allowed some of the former officials who had been carried off to the rebel court to get away and return to Ch'ang-an. Among them was Tu Fu's friend, Cheng Ch'ien. There is a poem by Tu Fu, describing their glad reunion. His friend's escape from Lo-yang may perhaps have encouraged Tu Fu to attempt to reach Su-tsung's headquarters, which in early March had been moved to Feng-hsiang, some one hundred miles due west of Ch'ang-an. Probably sometime in May, Tu Fu made the hazardous journey through or round the rebel lines to Feng-hsiang. He described his emotion at safely completing his escape in the three-poem series *Rejoicing to have Reached the Traveling Court.*

I

Westward, I yearned for news from Ch'i's south side,
But none returned again from there.
With starting eyes I faced the setting sun;
My heart died and became cold ashes.
Misty trees led me on my way;
Linked hills suddenly opened to my gaze.
My friends wondered to see me aged and thin;
With what hardship I had come from the rebels.

II

I sadly brooded in the Tatar pipe-filled evening;
Chilling was spring in the Han garden.
To have come back alive is but today a fact;
As I went on byways, I was living by moments.
When I first saw the ceremonies of the Commandant of Services,
I knew that the aura of Nan-yang had been renewed.
My rejoicing heart is utterly overwhelmed;
Sobbing, I soak my kerchief with tears.

III

Had I died, who would have reported it?
Now I have come back, I start to pity myself.
I still gaze at T'ai-po's snow;
I rejoice to face the Wu-kung sky.
My shadow is at rest among the thousand officials;
My heart revives before the seven commanders.
Today I know that for the nation of Han
This can be counted a restoration year.[15]

Tu Fu's arrival at the "traveling court" (an expression generally used in whatever circumstances the emperor was away from his capital) was to expose him to dangers of another sort. He was given the appointment of *Tso shih-i* ("Omissioner"[16] of the Left), a not very high-ranking post in the imperial Chancellery, which carried the duties of bringing to the emperor's notice matters that had in some way been overlooked or mishandled. Tu Fu with a rapid but ill-judged display of zeal in his new office came to the defense of Fang Kuan, who had incurred the heavy defeats at Ch'en-t'ao and Ch'ing-fan. In spite of these, Fang Kuan had been allowed to continue as a chief minister until June 757, when he was dismissed on a charge of associating with a musician who was said to have taken bribes to secure introductions to Fang Kuan for others. Tu Fu's memorial angered the emperor, who ordered his arrest and examination by a commission of ministers. It was found that although his words had been rash, he had not acted improperly, and on the recommendation of Chief Minister Chang Hao he was pardoned. Tu Fu's memorial of thanks for the emperor's forgiveness, which has survived, reveals his obstinate character rather than his political judgment.

While he was endangering his own life in his newly gained office, Tu Fu must have been extremely anxious for the safety of his wife and children. *To Describe My Feelings*, written at Feng-hsiang, portrays these anxieties.

Since last year, when T'ung-kuan was stormed,
My wife and children have so long been parted from me.
This summer, when plants and trees grew tall,
I escaped and managed to get away to the west.
In hemp sandals I had audience with the Emperor;
The sleeves of my robe revealed both elbows.
The court was moved that I had returned alive;
Relatives and friends grieved to see me old and wretched.
With tears I received the post of Omissioner;
To the fugitive the ruler's favor was generous.
Although I could have gone to my humble home,
I could not bear to make the request at once.
I sent a letter to seek news of San-ch'uan,
Not knowing whether they were there or not.
Recently I heard it too shared in the disasters;
The slaughter went even to fowls and dogs.
In the leaking thatched hut among the hills,

Does anyone lean by door or window?
Lying smashed at the foot of the green pines,
On the cold ground the bones may not have rotted.
How many of them have kept their lives?
A whole family surely could not be fortunate?
To that place of precipices and fierce tigers
With choking feelings I turn my head.
Since I sent my first letter,
It is now already ten months.
I have come to fear to have news;
What more can my heart bear?
The fortunes of Han now are restored;
In the past I was always fond of wine,
But I deeply brood at joyous gatherings,
And fear that I may be a lonely old man.[17]

Eventually a letter did come from his wife in Ch'iang Village
that they were all safe, and in September he was given leave to
visit them. He set out on foot on the first day of the intercalary
eighth month of the Chinese year (September 18), but he was
provided with a horse for the last two-thirds of the journey to
Fu-chou through the kindness of his host at Pin-chou, some
seventy miles northeast of Feng-hsiang. As *To Describe My Feelings* and other examples, quoted earlier, like *P'eng-ya Road*, have
shown, Tu Fu achieved some of his finest poetry in the description of his feeling for his family. He had a remarkably sure touch
in conveying the nature and quality of an emotion. *The Ch'iang
Village* series, written after his reunion with his family, is an expression of intense relief.

I

From west of the high-peaked red clouds
The sun's rays descend upon the level ground.
By the brushwood gate birds chatter;
A traveler has returned over a thousand *li*.
My wife and children wonder that I am here;
When their suprise is over, they still wipe tears.
In the age's disorder I was whirled away;
To come back alive by chance I've managed.
Our neighbors crowd the wall tops;
Moved to tears, they too are sobbing.
Late in the night again we take a candle,
And look at each other as if in a dream.

The second poem of the series introduces the thought that continually worried his mind in the years after 755. In misfortune he almost invariably felt that the sufferings of others must be greater; in times of happiness he often felt guilty, as if personal joys were improper in the disorder of the times.

II

An old man, I am troubled by my stolen life;
I hold small the joy of my homecoming.
My darling boy does not leave my knee;
He fears that I may go away once more.
I think of how last year we liked to seek the cool,
And so wandered round the trees beside the pond.
Now, howling, the north wind is strong;
Pondering my affairs, I am consumed by every sort of worry.
Happily I know that the millet has been harvested,
And am aware that the grain still is dripping
Since now there is sufficient to pour,
Let me with it console my evening.

III

All the fowls are cackling in confusion;
When visitors come, the fowls start fighting.
I chase the fowls up into the trees,
Then I hear the knocking at the brushwood gate.
Four or five old fellows have come
To ask after my long and distant travels.
In his hands each has his gift;
They pour flasks of cloudy and clear,
Deeply apologizing for the wine's poor taste.
"The millet ground has none to plow it;
There's still no end to the fighting;
The lads are all fighting in the east."
"Let me sing for you, old fellows.
In such hardship you shame me with your generosity."
When the song is ended, I look up to Heaven and sigh,
While from them all the tears stream down.[18]

At the same time that he produced this series of simple poems, Tu Fu was probably engaged upon one of his major works, the one hundred and forty-eight-line *The Journey North*, part travel poem, part poem of homecoming, part review of the war situation. The description of his homecoming is circumstantial and a triumph of realism.

I too fell into the Tatar dust;
Now I return, my hair quite white.
When, after a year, I reach the thatched house,
My wife's and my children's clothes are a hundred patches.
Our cries of grief, the sounds of the pines give back;
The mournful spring joins in our somber sobs.
The boy whom I always spoiled—
His face is whiter than snow.
At the sight of his father he turns away and cries;
He is dirty and without stockings on his legs.
In front of the bed are my two small daughters,
Whose patched clothes just cover their knees.
In the sea pattern there are gaps in the waves,
Filled with scraps from an old embroidered robe;
T'ien-wu and the Purple Phoenix
Are upside-down on their short dresses.
In the wretchedness of my feelings
I lie vomiting for several days.
"Surely I have silk in my bag
To save you shivering with cold!"
Powder and eyeblack are taken from their packages;
Coverlets are gradually opened out.
My poor wife's face regains its brightness;
My silly daughters try to dress their hair.
They imitate their mother in everything she does:
The morning makeup is liberally smeared;
Time after time they apply red powder;
All askew they paint broad eyebrows.
Now I have returned alive and am with my children,
I seem almost to have forgotten hunger and thirst.
Clamoring with questions, they struggle and pull my beard;
Who could shout at them to stop?
When I recall my sadness among the rebels,
I gladly accept all this confused hubbub.
Newly returned, for a while I let my mind be easy;
Just now could we bear to talk of how we are to live?[19]

No similar sustained description of a domestic scene can be
found in earlier Chinese poetry, and there are probably few to
parallel it in the work of later poets who had Tu Fu's example
before them. By this period in his life he had achieved complete
sureness, and he clearly set no limitations to the subject matter
of poetry. The manner in which in *The Journey North* he combined within one poem his personal acts and intimate concerns

with high matters of state may be seen as stemming from the subconscious awareness of the great poet that whatever he writes is inevitably public. On the other hand, the approach of *shih* poetry (in general contrast to *fu*) was essentially personal. The point of view was that of "I," however little the personal pronoun was used. However much he became the "poet-historian," Tu Fu never cast off the personal standpoint of *shih* poetry. Thus a long poem like *The Journey North* is really only an enlargement by many diameters of the more common short poem in which the personal and the public stand side by side in the space of a few lines.

The Recovery of the Capital

In his review of the war in *The Journey North* Tu Fu had shown a certain optimism: "As I sit, I feel the noxious influence is clearing." This optimism proved to be justified. On November 13 the T'ang forces inflicted a major defeat on the rebels near Ch'ang-an, and the capital was recovered. The following month Su-tsung returned from Feng-hsiang to receive news on the way of the recapture of Lo-yang. He made a triumphal entry, at which Tu Fu was apparently present, into the capital on December 8. His father Hsüan-tsung, the former emperor, also returned from Ch'eng-tu.

The rebellion seemed to be virtually ended. Shih Ssu-ming surrendered and was allowed to remain in the northern border-command of Fan-yang as governor-general. Only An Ch'ing-hsü held out in the city of Yeh (modern An-yang, Honan) and was not expected to resist for long. Rewards for service and punishments for disloyalty were now awarded.

Of Tu Fu's friends who had been captured and taken to the rebel capital in Lo-yang only Cheng Ch'ien fared badly. He was banished to a minor provincial post at T'ai-chou (modern Lin-hai, Chekiang) where he was to die. The two friends never met again. Wang Wei (701–61), one of the great T'ang poets and painters, whom perhaps he came to know well only at this time (he does not appear earlier in Tu Fu's poems) was demoted in office but still had a capital appointment. Su Yü escaped all blame and was given new office.

The unfortunate Li Po had been involved in March 757 in the revolt of one of Hsüan-tsung's sons, Li Lin, Prince of Yung, who had thought to take advantage of his appointment as governor-general at Chiang-ling (in modern Hupeh) to create an independent kingdom. By an unhappy chance, leading part of the forces sent against Prince Lin was Tu Fu's other companion in their former excursions in "Liang and Sung," Kao Shih, who had been made governor-general of Huai-nan. Li Po was eventually banished in the autumn of 758 to Yeh-lang in the far south.

Back in his post of omissioner, Tu Fu in the early months of 758 had the company of his old friend Ts'en Shen whom he himself had recommended in Feng-hsiang in the previous year. Ts'en Shen occupied a similar advisory post to his own, but in the Secretariat instead of the Chancellery.[20] Two newer friendships, formed in Feng-hsiang, with the writer Chia Chih and with the much younger Yen Wu, who was to be one of Tu Fu's most important patrons in his late years, could be maintained, for both were still in posts in the capital. As always, Tu Fu showed his great capacity for making new friendships as well as being steadfast in old ones, and so new names appear.

Among poems to friends and his contributions to the usual poetic exchange of poet-officials in the capital, he once again produced a longer poem reviewing the military and political situation, *Wash the Weapons and the Horses!*,[21] ending with a characteristic "How shall we get strong men to draw down the Heavenly River/To wash clean the weapons that they may long be unused?" In this eruditely allusive poem,[22] while he shares the general thankfulness at the restoration of the dynasty and the general belief that the rebellion was all but crushed, he displays some unease over political affairs. His fears are assumed to have been centered on the eunuch Li Fu-kuo, who was beginning to exercise a dominant and, from the viewpoint of regular government officials, improper influence over Su-tsung. Nevertheless, "Within the passes was kept a Chancellor Hsiao;/In the camp again was employed a Chang Tzu-fang." Under these names of Hsiao Ho and Chang Liang, the advisers of the founder of the Han dynasty, Tu Fu seems to refer to Fang Kuan, on whose behalf he had dangerously sought to intervene the year before, and Chang Hao, who had then counseled leniency toward the poet. They still had high office at the court, but soon were to fall and to bring Tu Fu's dismissal as their partisan.

There was no dramatic incident as in the previous year, and

indeed there is very little firm evidence of how things went with Tu Fu in his office during the first half of 758. There is a poem from his friend Ts'en Shen, which appears to enjoin caution upon him. He might be expected to be offering energetic, if unwelcome, advice to the throne. There are poems in which he describes himself working late at night or all night. On the other hand, there are self-accusations of negligence and implications of heavy drinking. Prices had risen very sharply with the economic dislocation of the rebellion, but Tu Fu's chief complaint was against the price of wine. He declares himself to have been a heavy drinker from his youth, and many references to drinking will already have been observed in the poems quoted. There is once again the problem of convention in the case of drinking as in many other aspects of Chinese writing. Chinese poets very generally represented themselves as heavy drinkers: it was the badge of the tribe. There is clearly much exaggeration, which brings with it the suspicion that the drinking may sometimes be as much symbolic as actual. If Tu Fu's proclaiming his drinking at this time has symbolic values, then he will be hinting at his dissatisfactions, for wine is that which "relieves care."

This year was to prove his last ever in Ch'ang-an, and in the spring he wrote a number of poems by the Curving Stream including two *lü-shih*, entitled simply *Curving Stream*, which in construction are very much in his late style with its experiments in unusual parallelisms. Had he known he was soon to leave his beloved city for the last time, he could hardly have written more tenderly.

I

Each petal that flies takes something away from spring;
The wind whirls ten thousand shreds just to make me sad.
Let me look at the flowers, soon to fall, before my eyes;
Let me not weary of the wine, sadness full, put to my lips.
In the little pavilion by the stream kingfishers nest;
On the high tomb at the garden's edge a unicorn sleeps.
Closely examine the principle of things and you must pursue
    happiness.
What use with fleeting name to fetter this body?

II

From the court returning, day after day I pledge my spring
    clothes;

And every day from the stream's bank I return quite drunk.
Wine debts commonly I have everywhere I go:
Men who live to seventy have always been rare.
Butterflies penetrate the blossoms to appear in their depths;
Dragonflies skim the waters in leisurely flight.
I send word to the spring scene: as we pass on together,
Let us for a while have joy together and not be parted.[23]

In the summer Chang Hao was sent from court to Ching-chou
(modern Chiang-ling, Hupeh), Fang Kuan to Pin-chou, and Yen
Wu to Pa-chou (modern Pa-chung, Szechwan). Chia Chih had
earlier been sent to Ju-chou (modern Lin-ju, Honan). Tu Fu
was banished to Hua-chou (modern Hua-hsien, Shensi), about
sixty miles east of the capital. Being of lesser rank than his
friends he received a subordinate prefectural appointment. His
duties were to oversee sacrificial ceremonies, schools, examinations and the periodic review of the services of the local officials.
He had reached Hua-chou by August 14, because in a poem with
that date he complains of the heat and the flies.

Though he also complains about the piles of documents to be
got through, he would have found at least one task to his taste.
Among his surviving prose works there is a plan for destroying
the remaining rebels, drafted by him on behalf of Prefect Kuo of
Hua-chou. Another interesting document to survive from this
period contains his questions on current problems set for the
prefectural examinations of 758.

At the end of October an attack on An Ch'ing-hsü was mounted
by imperial forces under the command of nine governors-general,
but whereas Prefect Kuo and Tu Fu's plan had called for the
attack to be made before the harvest, An Ch'ing-hsü was able to
withdraw into Yeh with stores of grain. The worst aspect of the
affair was that Shih Ssu-ming, who had been allowed to remain
in Fan-yang with his army intact, went once more into revolt.

In the twelfth month of this year (in the Western calendar
January 759) Tu Fu went on business, presumably of an official
nature, to Lo-yang. This gave him an opportunity at long last to
visit his old home at Yen-shih. Here he wrote several poems for
his brothers, of which two may be quoted.

Let me be glad that Ho-nan is pacified
And not enquire of the siege of Yeh City.

After a hundred battles who now is living?
For three years I have longed for your return.
In our old garden the flowers open by themselves;
In the spring days the birds still fly.
But smoke from men's houses has ceased:
From east to west news is rare.

Thinking of My Brothers II[24]

Who has succeeded in returning after the rebellion?
A strange place may be better than one's home.
It simply makes my heart bitter,
Since long I thought to live and die with you.
Your books remain still in the walls;
Your concubine has left the house.
The old dog knows my distress:
With lowered head it lies by my bed.

Getting News of My Brother[25]

For some there could never be a return, and in *He Will Not Return*[26] he lamented a cousin killed in the war.

Upon your face three years of dust,
While in spring air plants shoot again.

Yet the return home could bring happy encounters also. To describe his reunion with a very old friend, a recluse named Wei, he used the very simple style, which he had used in *P'eng-ya Road* and in parts of *The Journey North*, and which he was soon to use again in the famous series of poems which he wrote on the return journey from Lo-yang.

In our lives we are parted
Just like Orion and Lucifer.
So what a night is this
When we share this candle's light!
Youth and prime, how long are they?
The temples of both of us are white.
Enquiring for old friends, we find half are dead;
We cry out in surprise, our hearts on fire within.
How could I know it would be twenty years
Before I mounted your hall again?
When we parted then, you were not married;
Now your sons and daughters form up in line.
Gladly they pay their respects to their father's friend

And ask me from what quarter I have come.
Before question and answer are over,
The children have set out the wine.
In the night rain they cut spring leeks;
Fresh-steamed rice is sprinkled with yellow millet.
My host exclaims how hard it is to meet,
And at a single pouring lines up ten cups.
Ten cups for sure won't make me drunk,
But I am moved how your friendship has lasted.
Tomorrow we shall be parted by the mountains,
The world's affairs for both uncertain.[27]

The world's affairs were indeed uncertain. On April 7, 759, the huge imperial forces investing An Ch'ing-hsü were routed by Shih Ssu-ming and there were immediate fears of the disasters of 756 being repeated. Kuo Tzu-i, who had been one of the most successful of the T'ang generals in the earlier campaigns against the rebels, fell back with the remnants of his army to defend Lo-yang, from which officials and citizens started to flee. Kuo Tzu-i built up his position at Ho-yang, northeast of Lo-yang, which did not fall until six months later. After his victory Shih Ssu-ming had An Ch'ing-hsü killed and proclaimed himself emperor.

In the midst of this new crisis for the dynasty Tu Fu made his way back to his post at Hua-chou. This time he wrote of the fighting against the rebels, not from the viewpoint of a patriot anxious for victory or of an official offering tactical advice, but as if he were seeing it through the eyes of those who were themselves or whose husbands and sons were pressed into service. His six poems of this time, the three "officer" poems (*san li*) and the three "parting" poems (*san pieh*) are regarded as his most masterly expression of his sympathy for the common people. They are assumed to have been written spontaneously as a continuing series in the course of his journey from Lo-yang back to Hua-chou. One Chinese commentator wrote: "He composed poems from what he witnessed—and bequeathed tears for a thousand years."[28] It is possible to doubt that they were completely spontaneous: one of the six seems to refer to a different season of the year.[29] They have a definite unity and might have been written or polished after his return to Hua-chou. There is an understandable assumption by chronologists—but one suspects it must sometimes be false—that every Chinese poem was written at the immediate time suggested by internal reference, unless there is a positive statement of recollection of past events. Whatever the case, these six poems together provide a distinctive climax to this central period of his life. The three "officer" poems are each related to a particular place through which Tu Fu passed on his way to Hua-chou. Hsin-an was some twenty miles along the road from Lo-yang; Shih-hao was a village in the area of modern Shen-hsien.

The Hsin-an Officer

A traveler I go upon the Hsin-an road,
And hear the shouts of a soldiers' roll call.
If one asks the Hsin-an officer, he says:
"The district is small and has no more men.
A military order last night was sent
That next I should choose youths to go."
"The youths are very short and small,
How can they defend Our Majesty's cities?"
The plumper youths have mothers to see them off;
The thin youths are all by themselves.
The bright water in the evening flows eastward;
Amid the green hills still there are sounds of weeping.
"Don't wear out your eyes!
Restrain your tear's flood!
Though your eyes are worn to the bone,
Heaven and Earth will never have pity.
Our troops were besieging Hsiang-chou;
Day and night we expected it to fall.
Who would have thought the rebels so hard to gauge,
And that our retreating armies would lie scattered?
They are foraging near their former camps;
They are training troops near the old capital;
They dig trenches but not down to water;
Their duties in tending the horses are also light.
Besides the imperial armies are well disciplined;
Their care for their men is very clear.
You who see them off, don't weep tears of blood;
The minister is like a father or an elder brother."[30]

The T'ung-kuan Officer

The soldiers, how distressed they are!
Building walls on the T'ung-kuan road.
The big walls are stronger than iron;

The small walls over a hundred thousand feet!
If one asks the T'ung-kuan officer, he says:
"We repair the barrier against the Tatars again."
He asks me to dismount from my horse,
Points out to me the angle of the hills.
"Up to the clouds palisades have been set:
A flying bird could not get over them.
If the Tatars come, we'll just defend ourselves;
There should be no fear for the western capital.
You see, sir, how the strong points
Are so narrow as to admit but a single cart.
In times of trouble when long lances were raised,
From remotest ages one man has served for its defense.
Alas for the battle of the T'ao-lin
Where a million men were turned to fish!
Please charge the general defending the pass
To take care not to imitate Ko-shu![31]

The Shih-hao Officer

At evening I lodged in Shih-hao Village,
Where an officer was by night seizing men.
The old man climbed the wall and fled;
The old wife went to answer the door.
The officer cried—oh how angrily!
The wife cried—oh how bitterly!
I heard the wife advance to make her plea.
"Three sons were at the siege of Yeh.
From one son a letter has come
That two sons lately died in battle.
The survivor a while has snatched his life;
The dead are forever ended.
In the house are no more men;
Only a grandson at the breast.
The grandson's mother has not come out;
To see the officer she has no whole skirt.
This old woman, through her strength is faded,
Let her go with you, officer, tonight,
Urgently answering the call to Ho-yang,
For she still can cook a morning meal."
Late in the night the sounds of talking ceased,
But I seemed to hear weeping's stifled sobs.
At daybreak I went on my way,
And only of the old man took leave.[32]

CHAPTER 3

The Years of Fullness

I A Moment of Decision

BY THE SUMMER of 759 Tu Fu had returned to his post at Hua-chou, and by mid-autumn he had left it. He was now in his forty-eighth year, and the step he took was a turning point in his life. In his poetic career it was the point at which the later Tu Fu begins to be marked off from the earlier. The great bulk of his surviving poetry dates from the last twelve years of his life.

The biography of Tu Fu in the *Hsin T'ang-shu* (*New T'ang History*) makes his decision to leave his office one forced upon him by the prevailing famine in the area. While his poem *Sighing on a Summer Day*[1] gives support to the existence of a drought during the summer of this year, all the other evidence indicates that it was the disappointment of his hopes for a public career, which sent him westward away from the capital on the beginning of a journey that was never to bring him home. The message of the short poem *Written on the Day After the Beginning of Autumn*[2] July 30 is quite clear.

> Days and months do not spare us;
> The seasons divided last night.
> Dark cicadas drone ceaselessly;
> Autumn swallows seem already about to go.
> All my life I have had a wish "to walk alone,"
> And I grieve that my years are half a hundred.
> To give up office is in one's own hands;
> What use is cramping service?

Once more he was beginning to talk of hermitage, and he took his family first to Ch'in-chou (modern T'ien-shui, Kansu) more than three hundred miles west of Hua-chou. Ch'in-chou was an important town in the eastern part of the border of command of Lung-yu, whose governor-general had the duty of holding back the incursions of the Tibetans. Why did Tu Fu come to this remote place? The debacle of the imperial armies and the uncertain situation which followed it clearly prevented him from going home to Yen-shih. In a poem which he wrote to Kao Shih and Ts'en Shen[3] from Ch'in-chou he said that he had not the money to live in the capital. Ch'in-chou seems to have become something of a refugee center at this time. A cousin, Tu Tso, had settled here, and he also found here an old Ch'ang-an friend in the Buddhist monk, Abbot Tsan. In the first of the twenty-poem series, *Miscellaneous Poems of Ch'in-chou* he writes: "Relying on others, I have made a distant journey."[4] This perhaps indicates that he had been positively urged to go to Ch'in-chou.

His response to this border city, set among "ten thousand mountain-folds," was mixed. The isolation depressed him, although at times he felt exhilaration at the wild scenery. He was immediately conscious of the threat posed by the Tibetans to the embattled empire, even though for the moment Lung-yu was undisturbed. He describes expeditions with his friend Abbot Tsan in search of a site for a "thatched hut," and he speaks admiringly of the valley where his cousin lived. Yet his apparent plan to settle at Ch'in-chou came to nothing, and after about two months he moved on. The poem *Leaving Ch'in-chou* expresses his forward hopes and sums up his reasons for leaving.

> In my decline I am lazier and more stupid;
> And my life is by me unplanned.
> When I've no food, I enquire for a fertile region;
> When I've no clothes, I think of a southern district.
> In Han-yüan at the beginning of the tenth month
> The weather should be like a cool autumn;
> The plants and trees should not have shed their leaves;
> I have heard too of the landscape's secret beauty.
> The name of Chestnut Pavilion besides is lucky,
> And below it there are excellent fields.
> To fill one's belly there are plenty of yams;
> Cliff honey also can easily be found;
> The thick bamboos, again, will have winter shoots;
> On clear lakes it will be possible to take a boat.
> Though I am troubled at so remote a lodging,
>   I must continue my past wanderings.

This place lies near a main highway;
Truly I fear the complexities of man's affairs.
To be sociable is not in my real nature;
To go to see the views does not relieve my cares.
In the mountain valleys there are no strange rocks;
The frontier fields only begin to give light crops.
How can it give consolation to an old man?
I'm disappointed but I may not linger here.
The sun disappears behind the lonely fort;
The cries of rooks fill the city walls.
In the middle of the night we urge our carts away;
We water the horses at a cold pond.
A profusion of stars and moon high above;
In the distance clouds and mists drift.
Enormous is the universe!
My road goes on and on forever.[5]

His new destination, Chestnut Pavilion, was near T'ung-ku
(modern Ch'eng-hsien, Kansu). Perhaps when he wrote the name
was "lucky," he was thinking of T'ao Yüan-ming's Chestnut Village. The famous hermit-poet (lived 365–427) was much in his
thoughts; there are many direct and indirect references in the
poems of this period. The place turned out to be less propitious
than its name. There were no yams; only acorns of the chestnut
oak. Hunger and want make their appearance in the poems, and
in a month Tu Fu and his family were once more heading south.

There was a worthy who "did not blacken his chimney";
There was a sage who "did not warm his mat."
The less should I, a hungry and foolish man,
Be able still to enjoy a quiet abode.
When first I came among these mountains,
I stopped my carriage and delighted in the remoteness.
How can I help that driven by things' complexity,
In one year I have made four journeys?
Uneasily I leave this remote place;
Uncertainly again I journey far.
I halt my horse among Dragon Pool's clouds;
I turn my head to the Tiger Cliff's rocks.
At the road's fork I take leave of several gentlemen;
As I clasp their hands, once more my tears fall.
Our association was not old or deep;
But for a lonely old man it is very sad.
My lifelong lazy and clumsy thoughts

Had chanced upon a spot to rest and hide.
Going and staying are both contrary to my wish;
I look up with shame at the birds' wings among the trees.

Leaving T'ung-ku[6]

With this fourth journey in a single year Tu Fu was beginning to represent himself as a perpetual traveler. His capacity for self-dramatization, as the last poem shows, was being called into vivid play. He was no doubt genuinely worried at his situation, but at the same time the poet in him had been highly stimulated by this new turn in his life and his entry into these border lands. These five months at the end of 759 contribute about one hundred and twenty poems to the extant collection. The number of poems which anthologists select from this time tends to be high, for the element of universality is generally present. There are distinctive features and themes, so that the work of the period has the character of a separate collection, and groups within it, such as the travel poems,[7] have a particular identity. From a view of Tu Fu's whole career, these five months can be seen to open a new phase in his poetry and in his essential attitude to poetry. The division seems sufficiently clear-cut for one to feel that the poet himself was intuitively aware of a significant change in his life and was subconsciously responding to it.

A first problem for him was justification of the step he had taken, and one of his several series entitled *To Express My Feelings*[8] of this period treats five "retired scholars" of the past and of his own time. It has been suggested already that Tu Fu was temperamentally unfitted for the hermit role, and he must himself have been aware of it. When he writes of hermits and hermitage his anxieties are fairly patent.

I

A hibernating dragon sleeps for three winters;
An old crane yearns for ten thousand *li* flight.
The worthy men of former times
Were ill-fated just as now.
Hsi K'ang died before his time,
But K'ung-ming found one who appreciated him.
They can compare with the pines on the slopes,
Whose use depends on their being sought.
Mighty are their trunks in frost and snow;
Yet with long years they become dead trees.

Both Hsi K'ang (223–62) and Chu-ko Liang (K'ung-ming; 181–234) were called "sleeping dragons," men who bided their time, but clearly Tu Fu is writing of himself also in the opening lines. He obviously had not abandoned the thought of a new "soaring." His fears that it might not be granted to him come out in the image of the dead tree, which is recurrent in his poems at this time.

In the third poem of the series, in which, unusually, he takes up a slightly reproachful attitude to T'ao Yüan-ming (T'ao Ch'ien) there is another example.

III

> T'ao Ch'ien was a recluse from the world,
> But he could not necessarily achieve the Way.
> When one reads the collection of his poems,
> One finds him often grieving to be sear and dry.
> His understanding of life was surely insufficient;
> His secret appreciation did not come early.
> Whether his sons were wise or foolish,
> Why did he trouble his heart?

This could be rather deceptive about Tu Fu's position, if one did not read it along with other poems of the same time. He seems to take T'ao Yüan-ming to task for failing to live up to his philosophy of acceptance of things as they are. For Tu Fu, who never accepted things as they were, this can only be an oblique way of rejecting hermitage for himself. The case is much more plainly put in another *To Express My Feelings* poem—the third of a three-poem series.[9]

> Who shall say that the harvest is late?
> Timely moisture does not have to be early.
> For the plowed fields the autumn rain was enough;
> The millet already is gleaming by the road.
> Spring's shoots, at ninth month's beginning,
> Have darkened in color with the sun's aging.
> I urge you, scholars in retirement,
> Not to grieve to be still sear and dry.
> The time will come to put forth your powers;
> Whether early or late is not ill or fair.
> Only I wonder at the Old Man in the Deerskin,
> Who forgot the world in front of his magic plant.[10]

To Tu Fu with his perennial hopefulness the old men who sat in gentle despair were irritating. They appear again in the seventh of the *Seven Songs Written While Lodging at T'ung-ku:* [11]

> A man who has not made a name, whose body is already old,
> For three years in hunger I have walked wild mountain ways.
> Among Ch'ang-an's ministers are many young men:
> Riches and honors must be striven for early.
> The scholars among the mountains, my old friends,
> Only talk of the past and have hurt feelings.

This reiterated emphasis on the "sear and dry" by a man well into middle age, who at least affected to believe that he had achieved nothing, must evoke sympathy for his defiant spirit. Though he had withdrawn from office, he had not abandoned hope, and certainly had not withdrawn from his old concerns. The first two poems of the series *To Express My Feelings* from which the third has been quoted above return once again to the pity of war. They both show the ever increasing breadth of his sympathy: war was terrible not only for Han Chinese but for all people.

I

> I dismount from my horse on an old battlefield;
> In every direction only an empty waste.
> The wind is sad; the clouds drift away;
> Yellow leaves fall in front of me.
> The rotting bones are bored by ants,
> And bound by creeping plants besides.
> Old men pass by and sigh:
> "The men of today still extend the borders."
> Han and barbarian in turn conquer,
> But the frontier never endures.
> Where can we find a General Lien P'o? [12]
> That the armies might all sleep in peace.

II

> In high autumn I climb the border mountains,
> And gaze southward to Ma-i Prefecture.
> The subjected barbarians are in the east fighting Tatars;
> Not one ablebodied man has been left behind.
> Their yurts are desolate and lonely,
> Overtopped by sad moving clouds.
> The old and feeble weep by the roadside,
> And long to hear the fighting's stopped.

> At Yeh things go this way and that,
> But the dead are piled in mounds.
> The generals have been already honored;
> How to bring aid, who can advise?

These two poems are a response to a scene immediately before his eyes, but they are also examples of a somewhat more reflective spirit. Conspicuous among the poems of this period are the sixteen *yung-wu* poems, which seem also the result of this increasingly reflective attitude. *Yung-wu* ("singing of things"; "things" include both animate creatures, plants and trees, and inanimate objects) was a long-established genre in Chinese poetry. Such poems were seldom purely descriptive, but contained a greater or lesser element of allegory. They thus provide a rich field of speculation for the commentator. In view of the indissoluble bonds of literature and politics in Chinese society, political references, which is suspected everywhere, is especially discovered in *yung-wu* poems, where it is least susceptible of confident affirmation or disproof. Whatever the nature of the allegory in this group of Tu Fu's poems,[13] his writing of them at this time does exemplify the change that was coming over his poetic career. Poetry now became a much larger part of his life. It can be said he became much more the professional poet. He both turned his whole life into poetry and adopted a more experimental attitude to its writing.

At this critical moment his thoughts turned to his family and his friends. His separation from his brothers troubled him even more now that he was "at the end of the world" in Lung-yu, and he wrote three poems in different forms but of similar content during this period. *Thinking of My Brothers on a Moonlit Night*[14] may represent his feeling.

> The guard tower drum puts an end to men's passing;
> In the frontier autumn—a single wild goose's cry;
> The dew from this night begins to whiten;
> The moon is as bright as it is at home.
> I have brothers but they are scattered;
> I have no home to ask if they are alive or dead.
> Their letters for long have not reached me;
> Worse still there's no end to the war!

He addressed a long poem of a hundred lines to his "fellow partisans" in Fang Kuan's group, Chia Chih and Yen Wu, in which, after reviewing the past three years and counseling his friends to be cautious, he ends on a rather pessimistic note. He suggests that his own career is ended and complains of the effort of writing long poems. One can have no idea of the order of composition, but in fact he wrote two other long double-addressee poems in Ch'in-chou, each of sixty lines, one to Hsüeh Chü and Pi Yao and the other to Kao Shih and Ts'en Shen. Another friend, Chang Piao, was also the recipient of a sixty-line poem. Most of the chronologists make the list of poems to friends still longer by the addition of four poems to Li Po and two to Cheng Ch'ien. One of the Li Po poems, *At the Sky's End Thinking of Li Po* from its title and content clearly belongs to this time. The others seem more likely to have been written in the previous year.[15] The two poems[16] to Cheng Ch'ien give no clue to where Tu Fu was at the time of writing, so that they cannot be firmly dated. It is certainly likely that when Tu Fu was writing so generally to or of his friends, he would have included Cheng Ch'ien, but these two poems could as well have been written in 758 or at any time before Cheng's death in 762.

Even when the poems of doubtful dating are excluded, the output of this short period was remarkable. Uncertainty and anxiety did not inhibit the flow of Tu Fu's brush.

II   *The Thatched Hut*

Tu Fu started out with his family from T'ung-ku on the first day of the twelfth month (December 24, 759) and they apparently completed the five hundred often hazardous miles to Ch'eng-tu in about a week. For in the poem *Ch'eng-tu City*, with which he marked his arrival at the "Southern Capital," he refers to the last month of winter and to the new moon being low in the sky.

> Shaded, the sun among the mulberries and elms;
> It shines on my traveler's clothes.
> I have journeyed over hill and stream's strangeness,
> And suddenly am at one corner of the sky.
> I shall meet none but new people;
> I cannot tell when I shall see my home.
> The Great River flows away to the east;
> Long is the time I have been a wanderer.
> The layered walls are filled with splendid houses;

In winter's last month the trees are green.
Bustling is this famous city,
Where pipes' sounds are spaced by reed organ notes.
Of true beauty but unpleasing to me;
I turn away and gaze at the river bridge.
Rooks and sparrows at night all return,
Yet the Central Plain is distant and dim.
The new moon does not climb high;
The host of stars still disputes its light.
From of old there have been travelers;
Why should I so bitterly grieve?[17]

Though he had now reached almost the furthest point in his travels and his homesickness was extreme, he was about to enjoy two or three years of almost happiness. These are the years of Tu Fu's version of the pastoral: the years of the thatched hut.

He was to settle not in the bustling city of Ch'eng-tu (lately dignified by the title of "Southern Capital," because of Emperor Hsüan-tsung's stay there) with its "ten myriad households," but in a place of "two or three families" in the southwestern outskirts of the city by the Brocade or Flower-Washing Stream. The only reliable source for where and by whose aid Tu Fu built the Thatched Hut is his own poetry and this does not provide complete and clear answers. It is very improbable that the site has been correctly identified during the last thousand years or that the present successor of a line of "Tu Fu's Thatched Huts" is on the original spot. From the titles of various poems the names of some of those who contributed to the building of the house and the setting out of the garden are known, but the identity of the "patron" in *Choosing a Dwelling* remains uncertain.[18]

By the Flower-Washing Stream and to the west of it,
My patron has chosen for me the secret beauty of wood and pool.
Already I knew, out of the city, there were few worldly affairs;
Besides there is a clear stream to dispel a stranger's grief.
Innumerable dragonflies, flying level, rise and descend;
A pair of ducks together dive and swim.
One can travel east ten thousand *li* at will;
If one needs to go to Shan-yin, one boards a little boat.[19]

By the late spring of 760 the building was finished and he could move with his family from the Buddhist monastery in which they had been staying.

With its back to the city my hut is finished and covered with white
   reeds;
One goes by the well-worn river path, down through the green out-
   skirts.
The *ch'i* tree groves keep off the sun with their leaves where the wind
   sings;
Big bamboos mingle in the mist with their stems from which the dew
   drips.
For a while stay the flying crows, leading their brood;
Continually come the chattering swallows, making new nests.
A bystander might mistakenly compare it to the house of Yang Hsiung,
But in my sloth I have no intention of writing a *Defense Against
   Ridicule*.[20]

Yang Hsiung (53 B.C.–18A.D.) was a native of Ch'eng-tu, and
the *Defense Against Ridicule* was an *apologia* for his going into
retirement and writing the *Great Mystery Classic* (*T'ai-hsüan
ching*). Tu Fu was perhaps obliquely declaring that he was not
really in retirement. The suggestion (with possibly the same
implication) that he was writing a *Mystery Classic* had been
made earlier in this year in a poem to him by his friend Kao Shih,
and rejected in his reply.[21] If this is the point of the reference, on
another occasion he expressed himself differently. In *I Have
Become a Farmer* he seems to profess his intention to grow old as
a farmer, dropping himself from the highest to the second of the
four classes of Confucian society.

> The Brocade City lies beyond the smoke and dust;
> The river village has eight or nine houses.
> Round lotuses float their small leaves;
> Fine wheat droops down its light ears.
> I have chosen a dwelling from now to grow old in;
> I have become a farmer, remote from the capital.
> Yet I think back with shame to the Magistrate of Kou-lou,
> For I am not able to seek after cinnabar.[22]

Even here he reproaches himself for being unlike the famous
alchemist Ko Hung (234–305), who in his old age asked for an
appointment in the far south where he could get cinnabar for his
pursuit of the elixir of immortality.
   With the fighting continuing in the north, one could not expect Tu Fu to put aside his anxieties for the country or for his
brothers, of whom he had no news. These anxieties still occupy

part or the whole of many poems of the first "Thatched Hut" period (760–mid 762). Yet this was the happiest period in the last decade of his life and is especially marked by nature poems and poems in praise of the simple life of the rustic hermit. The rise in the numbers of *lü-shih* (regulated verse), with an increasing experimentalism, shows how much poetry had become his principal preoccupation.

A curve of the clear river flows around the village;
The long summer day, everything in the village has secret beauty.
As they please, come and go the swallows in the roof;
Closely flock together the gulls in the water.
My wife makes a chessboard by painting paper;
My boys make fish hooks by bending needles.
What an often sick man needs is only medicines;
Beyond these what should an insignificant person seek?

The River Village[23]

Here again, as in *Choosing a Dwelling*, Tu Fu uses his favorite term *yu* (rendered "secret beauty," as he uses it to describe scenery, whether natural or man-aided, which is beautiful yet hidden, remote or in some manner out of the way) to set his highest seal of approval on his new home. The restless spirit—it is interesting to note that he often calls himself "lazy" at this time—was almost captured by the quiet beauty of the summer village and could, like his hermit-mentor T'ao Yüan-ming, show delight in the company of his family in a rustic setting. *Aboard a Little Boat* has several reminiscences of T'ao's poems.

Staying a while in the Southern Capital, I plow the southern acres;
Wounded in spirit by gazing north, I sit in the northern window.
In the daytime I lead my wife aboard a little boat;
In the fine weather we watch the children bathe in the clear river.
Flying together, butterflies always chase one another;
Single-stalked lotus blossoms naturally pair.
We have brought what tea and sugar cane juice we have;
Our earthen pots do not yield to jars of jade.[24]

But what sort of farmer was Tu Fu? "I plow the southern acres" is a literary reference to indicate his hermit condition, and no doubt "I have become a farmer" must be similarly understood. The little "begging" poems, written early in 760, were for shade trees, bamboos, and fruit trees for the garden, and he writes

proudly in *A Visitor*:[25] "I have hoed with my own hand the thin
vegetable shoots;/Let me pluck a few for the sake of our friendship." Beyond a little gardening and some suggestion of fishing,
there is no evidence for Tu Fu attempting to feed himself and his
family either by his own hand or by hired help. The Thatched
Hut was the abode of a "withdrawn" gentleman, not a gentleman
farmer. The clearest indication of this is given in the poem *To Be
Inscribed on My Thatched Hut Beyond the River*, written in 763
at Tzu-chou.

> I was born with a nature unrestrained;
> I constantly desire to escape to Nature.
> I am fond of wine and love wind blown bamboos;
> When I choose a dwelling, it must have woods and a spring.
> Encountering disorder, I came to the river in Shu;
> Suffering sickness, I followed what suited me.
> We cleared the weeds first from a single *mou*;
> Then we just continued to widen the land.
> The work began in *Shang-yüan*,
> And came to an end in *Pao-ying*.
> Dared I plan for the building to be beautiful?
> Yet I recognized that the situation was good.
> Terraces and pavilions followed the lie of the land;
> The spaciousness accorded with the clear river.[26]

After he had moved into the Thatched Hut, he was probably
very little less dependent on others for sustenance than when he
had been living in the monastery and a friend had "provided rice
from his salary." When funds or supplies ran low he would become alarmed and the worry would always turn into poetry. An
example is the song *Hundred Anxieties*.

I remember in my fifteenth year my heart was still childish;
Strong as a brown calf, I ran to and fro.
When pears and dates ripened in the courtyard in the eighth month,
In a single day I could climb the trees a thousand times.
Now all of a sudden I am in my fiftieth year;
I sit and sleep much and seldom walk or stand.
I force myself to joke for my hosts' sake,
Yet grieve to see a hundred anxieties gather about my life.
When I go in at my gate, still there is scarcity within my walls.
My wife sees the same expression upon my face.
My foolish children are ignorant of proper manners;
With angry cries they demand food and weep at the kitchen door.[27]

Occasionally too, he lets one see the approach (or reproach) direct to his friends, as in *A Quatrain Sent to Kao Shih, Prefect of P'eng-chou Through Censor Ts'ui.*

> Of my hundred years half are already gone;
> Autumn comes, yet brings hunger and cold.
> Ask the Prefect of P'eng-chou for me
> When he will relieve my distress.[28]

Not only were friends sometimes slow to help, but nature also might deal unexpected blows to shatter the rural peace. A summer storm uprooted the ancient *nan* tree which had influenced the choice of the site for the Thatched Hut.

> By the river stood a *nan* tree in front of my thatched hut;
> Old folk told me that it was two hundred years old.
> It was entirely for this that I cleared and chose the site;
> In the fifth month I already imagined autumn cicadas.
>
> From the southeast came a whirlwind, shaking the earth;
> The river rose, rocks rolled, clouds scattered.
> The trunk still struggled to resist the storm;
> Did Heaven intend its roots to be torn from the depths?
>
> My nature loved the old tree by the blue waves,
> Spreading over the bank a green canopy.
> Peasants often lingered in fear of snow and frost;
> Passersby stopped to listen to its pipe-notes.
>
> A tiger toppled, a dragon overthrown, it lies in the brush;
> Tear tracks' bloody marks fall down my breast.
> When I have a new poem, where shall I recite it?
> The thatched hut now is without distinction.[29]

This *Song of My Nan Tree Uprooted by the Storm* will belong to 760, if the fourth line is understood, as seems necessary, that he had not actually heard the autumn cicadas in the tree.[30] It is generally placed with one of the most famous of all Tu Fu's poems, *Song of My Thatched Roof Shattered by the Autumn Wind.* There is probably no means of determining whether the latter is from the autumn of 760 or 761, but it is worthwhile to let the two stand together, as the comparison serves to bring out the much greater power of the second poem.

In the eighth month, height of autumn, the wind angry howled,
Unrolled from off my roof three layers of reeds.

The reeds flew over the river, strewed the river's edges:
High, they hung in the tall tree tops;
Low, they whirled in the deep pools.
From Southern Village gangs of boys cheat me in my age and infirmity;
Heartlessly to my face they play the thief;
Openly with armfuls, go off into the bamboos.
Till my lips are burning, my mouth parched, I shout to no end.
So I return, leaning on my stick and sighing to myself.
In a while the wind is still, the clouds ink colored;
The autumn sky silently approaches darkness.
My cotton quilt, after many years, is cold as iron;
My spoilt child, restless in sleep, trod the lining to shreds.
Over my bed the roof leaks; there is no dry place;
The streaming rain like hemp threads, never broken.
Since the rebellion seldom have I slept well:
The long night, soaked, how can I get through?
Where can I find a mansion of a million rooms?
To shelter every poor scholar, with a smiling face;
In wind and rain unmoved, secure as a mountain.
Oh when before my eyes there sprang up such a house,
Though my hut alone were smashed and I froze to death, I should
  be content.[31]

In spite of such a magnificent outcry against misfortune as this
—and Tu Fu had a great facility for variation in intensity—the
note of cheerfulness and near serenity was largely sustained
throughout this period. His hermitage, like T'ao Yüan-ming's, was
kept "near the city," and he was very far from being cut off from
social contacts, even if in some of the earlier poems of the period
he affects gratitude and surprise that he should receive visitors
in his "remoteness." He probably went quite often to the city and
there is evidence of visits to towns more or less distant from
Ch'eng-tu. There are several short poems, probably from 761,
which suggest some success in the stilling of the voice of his
Confucian conscience.

At Random

I

The country sunlight is limitlessly bright;
The spring waters are sparklingly clear.
Sand bank rushes are everywhere;
Village paths go from house to house.
I simply practice easygoing habits,

And always follow him who strained wine with his turban.
Before my eyes there are no vulgar things;
Though often sick, yet my body is light.

It was T'ao Yüan-ming who strained wine with his turban.

II

On the river bank it is already mid-spring;
Under the blossoms again it is dawn.
I lift my face and longingly look at the birds;
I turn my head and imagine I answer someone.
In my reading difficult words are passed over;
In my drinking full jars are frequent.
My new friend, the old man of O-mei,
Knows that my laziness is real.[32]

At other moments, however, he raises doubts that his laziness
was real, for he protests too much.

I walk in clogs the deep wood's evening;
I open the jar to linger drinking alone.
Bees on their backs cling to fallen catkins;
Ants in column climb the rotting pear tree.
My worthlessness shames me before true retirement;
But in a secluded spot I can find instant happiness.
I have no aspiration to "cap and carriage";
It is not that I am proud of my present state.
Drinking Alone[33]

Even if one may see that the hermit role is a little too consciously assumed and that the repeated "desire to escape to
Nature" is finally unconvincing, Tu Fu responded easily to this
new chapter in his experience and gave to it his own individual-
ity. The social poems of this period find their context and color in
his immediate surroundings, while the underlying attitude and
sympathies remain unchanged. *Diseased Tangerines* and *Rotten
Coir Palms* are the most often cited of a number of poems with
similar titles. Tangerines were a special tribute sent to the court
from the area in which he was living, but presumably they stand
as a symbol of protest against any form of luxury in these difficult
times.

All the tangerine trees help us little:
Many though they are, what's their use?
Alas! their fruits are small

And bitter as wild plums.
Cut open, full of maggots;
To pick them is purposeless.
Since they are quite unfit to eat,
Should one simply save the skins?
Miserable, their half-dead leaves
That can't bear to leave their branches:
In black winter piled with frost and snow
And blown by gales besides.
I have heard that in the P'eng-lai Palace
Were rows of Hsiao-Hsiang trees.
This fruit does not crop every year,
So its glow was missing from the imperial table.
When, since rebels still rampage,
Our ruler is curtailing luxuries,
Your disease is Heaven's intent;
Yet I fear the officials may be blamed.
I remember how the messengers from Nan-hai
Galloped to present lichees.
Hundreds of horses died on mountain and in valley;
Even now old men grieve over it.[34]

The coir palm equally must stand as a particular symbol of the general hardships of the people of "the Kiang and Han" (modern Szechwan) under the pressure of military demands. In "the dead now are already ended; How shall the living save themselves," his *Shih-hao Officer* is recalled.

In Shu there are many coir palms:
Eight or nine of every ten are tall.
Their fronds are continually stripped,
So, though numerous, they easily rot.
Vainly they spread their cloudlike leaves,
Green even when the winter has come.
Axes lay on from every side,
And they decay sooner than water willows.
I grieve for the times and regret the army's needs,
For which things may be wholly seized by officials.
Oh, you men of the Kiang and Han,
What is left of the things you have grown or made?
You are like the rotten coir palms,
Which long have given me deep sighs.
The dead now are already ended;
How shall the living save themselves?

> Dolefully the orioles cry;
> I turn to see autumn down float by.
> I think of your withered forms,
> Lying broken among the thorns and tares.[35]

While the great rebellion in the north was still not repressed, Tu Fu in his retreat in the southwest now witnessed examples of the type of local military revolt which was frequent during the latter half of the T'ang period. The practice which was followed after the outbreak of An Lu-shan's rebellion of appointing local governors-general with military forces under their control throughout the country as well as in the frontier regions opened the way for these governors-general or their subordinates to seek independence. The revolt of Prince Lin in which Li Po was involved was an early case. On June 5, 761 the prefect of Tzu-chou (modern San-t'ai, Szechwan), Tuan Tzu-chang drove out his superior, Governor-General Li Huan, from Mien-chou (modern Mien-yang, Szechwan), declared himself prince of Liang, and renamed Mien-chou, Lung-an fu. The revolt was put down in a fortnight by the assistance of the forces of the Ch'eng-tu governor-general, Ts'ui Kuang-yüan. Tu Fu commemorated the events in *Playful Song for the Noble Hua.* Hua Ching-ting was a subordinate commander of Ts'ui Kuang-yüan's troops which looted Mien-chou with great violence.

> Among the fierce captains of Ch'eng-tu is the noble Hua,
> Whose name small children, learning to talk, know.
> When he is used like a swift falcon, wind and fire arise;
> Let the rebels he meets be many, his heart is at once light.
> When the Vice-Governor of Mien-chou donned the yellow,
> Our noble Hua swept him away and subdued him in a day.
> Tzu-chang's head, obscured with blood,
> He picked up and threw before Governor Ts'ui.
> Lord Li again had his governorship,
> And men said our noble Hua was unequalled in the world.
> Since he is declared unequalled in the world,
> Why does the Emperor not summon him to capture the Eastern
>   Capital?[36]

Violence against the inhabitants of captured cities by rebel or loyalist forces became a common occurrence, as fighting continued. Though Tu Fu does not refer to it here directly as he does elsewhere, the tone of this "playful" poem is clearly critical. On this occasion an official inquiry was held. What happened to Hua Ching-ting is unknown, but Governor-General Ts'ui Kuang-yüan died of worry in November and was subsequently replaced by Tu Fu's friend Yen Wu.

The year 762 should, therefore, have been a fortunate one for Tu Fu, and in the early months the promise seemed fair. Yen Wu was kind to the poet, who probably hoped for an advisory post on his staff. In May the former emperor Hsüan-tsung died, and a fortnight later the Su-tsung emperor died amid a struggle for power between his empress and the eunuch Li Fu-kuo. Li Fu-kuo emerged victorious and set on the throne the heir-apparent, known to history by his posthumous name of Tai-tsung. Yen Wu was called to the capital and Tu Fu accompanied him all the way to Mien-chou to see him off. In *Ten Rhymes to Speed His Excellency Yen on His Way to Court* he perhaps sees in the hope of a court appointment for his friend the chance of his own return to the capital.

> How should I spend the old age of my life in Shu?
> If I do not die, I may have the chance to return to Ch'in.
> If Your Excellency should rise to a Chief Ministry,
> Do not be careful of yourself in the face of danger![37]

In his final farewell poem, however, he strikes a very melancholy note, which moved the commentator P'u Ch'i-lung to remark that one does not know whether it is written with ink or tears.

> Far have I escorted you and now take leave;
> Amid the green hills vain are my feelings.
> For when shall we take up our cups again,
> And walk together under last night's moon?
> Every prefecture sings a song of regret;
> For three reigns you have had honors in court and province.
> To the riverside village I return alone,
> In silence to support my remaining life.
>
> *Four Rhymes Again to Speed His Excellency*
> *Yen at Feng-chi Post Station.*[38]

The melancholy was appropriate for reasons Tu Fu did not yet know. He did not "return alone" to his village. The first "Thatched Hut" period was in fact ended.

III *In Flight Again*

Hardly had the friends parted than a revolt broke out in Ch'eng-tu, which prevented Yen Wu from proceeding to the capital and sent Tu Fu in flight to Tzu-chou. The chief leader of the revolt was Hsü Chih-tao, vice-prefect of Ch'eng-tu and probably the subject of a poem by Tu Fu, written earlier in the year.[39] Violent though this affair was, it seems not to have lasted more than about a month, but Tu Fu's absence from the Thatched Hut lasted until the spring of 764. After his return he wrote *The Thatched Hut*, the first part of which provides, together with his friend Kao Shih's memorial,[40] the contemporary record of this rebellion.

Before, when I left the thatched hut,
Barbarians had cut off Ch'eng-tu.
Now I have returned to the thatched hut,
Ch'eng-tu is just free of trouble.
Let me describe the beginning of the revolt,
When the upset came in a moment.
The Governor-General set out for the court;
A gang of subordinates began their fell designs.
At midnight they cut off a white horse's head;
Bound themselves with its blood in a clumsy fashion;
In the west took over the Ch'iung-nan troops;
In the north cut the road at the Sword Pass.
Some tens of officeless fellows
Thrust themselves into power in the cities.
Their situation did not admit of two leaders,
And we began to hear of strife between Han and barbarian.
The western troops then mutinied;
The rebel leaders slew each other.
How would one expect "elbow and armpit" quarrels;
That they would of themselves become owls and jackals?
All loyal men were deeply angered
That the rules of order were violently transgressed.
In one state there were in fact three rulers,
And ten thousand men were likely to become dead fish.
They matched each other in show of power;
Which was ready to consider the guiltless?
Before their eyes were set manacles and fetters;
Behind them reed organs and pipes played;
Chatting merrily they carried out executions;
Flowing blood filled the boulevards.

Still now at the places of execution
In a storm one may hear the wailing.
The concubines and horses of the dead
With sad faces satisfied their captors' pleasure.
When a country has laws and regulations,
Such things can cause alarm and distress.[41]

The early days of this rebellion were no doubt very alarming
for Tu Fu with his now long experience of such dangers, and he
would have been very concerned for his wife and children from
whom he again found himself separated. They seem soon to have
joined him in Tzu-chou, and, although there are some gloomy
lines, the winter of 762 passed quite happily for him. Who his
host was during his stay in Tzu-chou is unknown.

The news coming from north China was at last good. On
November 20, Shih Ch'ao-i, who had succeeded to the leadership
of the rebels, after effecting the murder of his father in 761, was
defeated near Lo-yang, and the eastern capital was recovered. The
city was brutally looted by the Uighur allies. Through the next
months the imperial armies advanced steadily and by February,
763, the An-Shih rebellion, which had lasted some seven years,
could be said to be ended. In Tzu-chou, Tu Fu rejoiced at the
news and thought that he could go home to Yen-shih.

Beyond the Sword Pass suddenly is reported the recovery of Chi-pei;
When I first hear of it, tears fill my robe.
I turn to look at my wife and children; where is their grief now?
Carelessly I roll up the *Songs* and *Documents;* my joy is almost mad.
In broad daylight I start to sing; I must indulge in wine.
With green spring for company, joyfully we'll go home.
At once from the Pa gorges we'll go through the Wu gorges,
Then down to Hsiang-yang and on to Lo-yang.

Hearing that the Imperial Armies Have
Recovered Ho-nan and Ho-pei[42]

This has been described as the happiest poem in Tu Fu's life.[43]
He did not, however, start out for home, but leaving his family
in Tzu-chou, he went to Mien-chou and thence westward to Han-
chou (modern Kuang-han, Szechwan). Here Fang Kuan had been
prefect since the autumn of 760, but had recently been called to
the capital. With the recall of both Yen Wu and Fang Kuan to
court, Tu Fu may well have felt that he too might be summoned

to an appointment. Fang Kuan did not in fact reach Ch'ang-an, but fell ill at Lang-chou (modern Lang-chung, Szechwan), where he died on September 15, 763. It was presumably Fang Kuan's illness and death that brought Tu Fu to Lang-chou from Tzu-chou where he had returned during the summer. On November 2, he made a sacrificial offering to Fang Kuan's spirit and wrote his *In Sacrifice for the Late Chief Minister, His Excellency Fang of Ch'ing-ho.*

A new danger was now looming for the empire—from the Tibetans whose menace Tu Fu had felt during his stay in Ch'in-chou in 759. An embassy, led by Tu Fu's friend Li Chih-fang, had been sent to them in June 763, but had been detained by them. In September they launched an invasion and rapidly took the northwestern frontier area of Lung-yu and began to press toward the capital, Ch'ang-an. The danger was concealed from the emperor by a new, powerful eunuch Ch'eng Yüan-chen (Li Fu-kuo had been murdered in the previous winter), and there were no forces assembled to defend the city. The emperor fled to Shen-chou (modern Shen-hsien, Honan) on November 16, and two days later the Tibetans entered to sack and pillage the city. Fortunately, Kuo Tzu-i came out of retirement to rally the imperial forces and retake the capital. The emperor returned to Ch'ang-an on February 2, 764.

The chronology of Tu Fu's movements during the later months of 763 is somewhat uncertain because there are difficulties in obtaining agreement between all the statements in his poems and other writings.[44] At some point he returned to Tzu-chou after receiving a letter from his wife that she was worried over the illness of one of their daughters, but probably before the end of January, 764, he was back in Lang-chou, together with his family, ready for a journey down the Yangste to the Southeast.

Tu Fu was very much concerned with the Tibetan invasion. Yet, though there are some examples of military advice such as the memorial he drafted for Prefect Wang of Lang-chou, one may detect in many of his poems of this time a prevailing note of war-weariness. He harps on the "ten years of fighting" and the overwhelming need for peace.

> In the whole world for ten years no end to fighting;
> The "dog warriors" are again at the capital's gates . . .
> Wolves block the roads and men have vanished;

Beacons light up the night; corpses lie this way and that.
The emperor must indeed be weary of fleeing;
The ministers truly ought to think of peace.
Only I fear there will be no change in demands on the people,
For I hear that evil favorites can keep their lives.
An old man by the river may err in his estimate;
His dull sight may not see the storm clearing.[45]

IV   *The Military Adviser*

In early 764 Tu Fu had definite plans to sail down the Yangtse.
He had apparently made arrangements for a relative[46] to take
care of the Thatched Hut. Even when a new appointment in the
prefecture of Ching-chao,[47] which would have taken him back
to Ch'ang-an, was given him, he declined it. Yet once again in the
end he did not go. The cause of the final change of mind was the
reappointment of Yen Wu to Ch'eng-tu as prefect and as governor-general of Chien-nan Province. So he took his family back to
the Thatched Hut.

I, poor wretch, had to flee;
For three years I gazed toward Eastern Wu.
But bows and arrows hid the Kiang and the sea;
It was hard to make an excursion to the Five Lakes.
I could not finally bear to leave here,
And came back to clear the overgrowth.
As I went in the gate, the four pines were there;
I walked in clogs among the myriad bamboos' thin stems.
The old dog was glad at my return;
He ran about under the skirts of my robe.
The neighbors were glad at my return;
They bought wine and brought it in bottles.
The great official was glad at my return;
He sent a horseman to ask what I needed.
The whole city was glad at my coming;
Visitors were crowded into the village.
The empire is still not at peace;
Stout lads are better than worthless scholars.
Drifting amid the wind and dust,
What place can be found for me?
In this time I appear a parasite,
But my bones' marrow is luckily not dried.
Food and drink will be a shame in my remaining life.
I'll eat ferns and not dare to go to excess.[48]

The exuberance of this second part of *The Thatched Hut,* even
in the closing declamation against his own uselessness, shows the
depth of his joy at having returned to this place which had come
to mean so much to him. As T'ao Yüan-ming had had five willows
and had named himself for literary tradition "The Gentleman of
the Five Willows", so Tu Fu in conscious imitation had planted
four pines in his hermit's garden. He had ended the poem *To Be
Inscribed on My Thatched Hut Beyond the River,* written at
Tzu-chou, with an expression of anxiety for the "four small pines."
Now on his return he found them flourishing and devoted a fine
poem to them, which reveals their talismanic significance.

> When the four pines were first transplanted,
> They would have been about three feet high.
> Since we parted three years have sped;
> In pairs they stand as tall as men.
> "If only I find them not uprooted,
> I shan't mind if the branches are withered."
> Their dark hue is fortunately flourishing;
> Their wide-spaced branches have a fine air.
> The small bamboo frames I had inserted
> Originally were in fact a protection,
> But in the end came to do harm,
> And I am shamed by a thousand yellow needles.
> Dare I be the master of an old grove,
> While the people are still not at peace?
> From fleeing rebels I have just now returned,
> When spring flowers fill my deserted home.
> As I survey the scene, I sigh at the disarray,
> But when I come to them, they comfort my sadness.
> They raise a cool breeze for me;
> It brushes my face like a light frost.
> They can be a support for my old age;
> I shall wait for their shade to spread.
> My life is without root or stem;
> Matched with you, I am indeed unstable.
> When I have a feeling, let me write my poem;
> Our situations can on both sides be forgotten.
> Do not boast that after a thousand years
> Your dark green will coil to the vaulted blue.
> *The Four Pines*[49]

Tu Fu many times in his poems expressed his longing for his
"old home" at Yen-shih, but, although he continued to write of

himself as only a sojourner in Shu, the Thatched Hut clearly came
nearest to being "home" for him in the long years of his late
wanderings. When he wrote: "Within my rural door I have kept
a resource for old age,"[50] he was considering the Thatched Hut in
material terms, and, since he left it in 765, never to return, in
material terms the remark proved untrue. In a spiritual sense,
however, one cannot doubt that the Thatched Hut was indeed a
resource which nourished the last ten years of his life.

Some time in mid-764 Yen Wu appointed Tu Fu to his military
staff. Such an appointment commonly was accompanied by the
granting of a non-active capital post, and Tu Fu was given the
title of Assistant Secretary of the Ministry of Works (*Kung-pu
yüan-wai-lang;* since, though nominal, this was his highest official
post, he is often referred to in Chinese as "Tu Kung-pu"). For
Tu Fu who had always displayed a keen interest in military matters the appointment should have been very welcome. Yen Wu
had the important task of removing the Tibetans from the western
prefectures of Chien-nan Province which they still occupied
(Tu Fu's friend Kao Shih had already failed in this task). The
desired appointment, however, seems to have come too late for
the poet, whose frequent poor health made a regular routine
burdensome—apart from the fact that only for very short periods
of his life can he ever have endured a routine. He was compelled
too to stay in the city, away from the Thatched Hut. *Spending
the Night at Headquarters,* written in the autumn of 764, breathes
an air of dissatisfaction.

> At the general's headquarters in clear autumn the *wu-t'ungs*
>   by the well are cold;
> As I pass the night alone in the river city, the candles burn low.
> While, the long night, horn notes wail, I mutter to myself;
> The beauty of the moon in the sky, who else watches?
> The wind and dust continue; news is cut off;
> The frontier is lonely; the roads are difficult.
> I have endured a state of distress for ten years;
> Now I am forced into the ease of "resting on a single branch."[51]

He felt himself also to be an object of suspicion or jealousy for
his younger colleagues and wrote plaintively in *Doubt Me Not!*[52]

> In the past my literary brilliance moved the ruler;
> Today hunger and cold dog the side of my way.

Late in life I offer a last fellowship to young men,
Who show affection to my face and laugh behind my back.

It seems that he often asked for leave from his office and at the
end of January, 765, he gave it up. Though there is one official
paper from this time preserved among his prose works, the poetic
record tilts more toward the private than the public side of his
life. The five-poem series *The River Village on a Spring Day* provides a summing-up of his time as a military adviser and his
second stay at the Thatched Hut, which were in the nature of an
interlude before his next great period, the K'uei-chou period.

I

Farming works in every village are urgent;
Spring waters by every bank are deep.
Of Heaven and Earth I have had a ten-thousand *li* view;
With the procession of the seasons come thoughts of one's "hundred
    years."
My thatched hut can still be a subject for poems;
The Peach Blossom Spring of course can be sought.
Difficulties have made me stupid at living;
I have drifted aimlessly until now.

II

From afar I have come to the Three Shu;
I have let six years slip away.
In my wandering existence I met an old friend;
Inspiration has come from woods and springs.
My excessive laziness accepts patched clothing;
On my many excursions I put up with holed shoes.
My boundary fence is no limit whatever;
I let my thoughts range over river and sky.

III

The bamboos I planted are a medley of green;
The peaches I trained are a blaze of pink.
The Stone Mirror moon passes into my heart;
The Snow Mountains wind reaches my face.
A red stemmed brush came with the ruler's command;
A silver tablet was given to an aged man.
Who expects, when his teeth are gone,
His name to be noted among those recommended?

IV

In sickness I wore the red seal ribbon;
Returning to rest, I pace the purple moss.
Within my rural door I have kept a resource for old age;
At headquarters I was ashamed before the many talents.
Beyond the swallows the sunlight's threads curl;
Beside the gulls the water-plant leaves open.
Neighbors send me fish and turtles,
And ask whether I can come often.

V

Rebel bands aroused Wang Ts'an's grief;
In middle years Master Chia was summoned.
By climbing a tower the one first wrote a masterpiece;
By the advancing of his place the other finally had honor.
Their dwellings have been noted in the records of former worthies;
Their talents made great their fame as recluses.
At other times I have cherished these two;
On this spring day again I brood on them.[53]

In this introspective series Tu Fu was again taking stock of his life, for he could not have imagined that much of his "hundred year" span remained. He was concerned for the name he would leave after his death; his thoughts turned often in this direction in his last years. If this concern now seems strange, it must be remembered that Tu Fu was a notable omission from anthologies of poetry made at the time. This would have made him conscious of the vagaries of fashion and taste. The examples of Wang Ts'an (177–217) and Chia I (died 169 B.C.) were pertinent to his own case. Wan Ts'an, like Tu Fu, had been a refugee through rebellion and had made his name by his *Teng-lou fu* (*Climbing the Tower*), which expresses his homesickness. The scholar and *fu*-writer Chia I, a native of Lo-yang, had been sent as Tutor to the Prince of Ch'ang-sha in the south, but late in his life he was recalled and honored for his opinions by .the emperor (who "advanced his place" in the court gathering). Tu Fu hoped that all the poetry which he had written as a sojourner in many places since 755 would secure his enduring fame and that he might even now be recalled to the court.

The deaths of his old friends Cheng Ch'ien and Su Yü in 764 may have combined with his own frequent illnesses to make a return home to Yen-shih seem urgent. The sudden death of

Yen Wu in May, 765 could provide an immediate reason for his departure from the Thatched Hut, but it is possible to argue that he left even before this event. The question is difficult to resolve. By July he had sailed down the Min River to Jung-chou (modern I-pin, Szechwan). Then he sailed on down the Yangtse, stopping at Yü-chou (modern Chungking) and Chung-chou (modern Chung-hsien, Szechwan), to reach Yün-an (modern Yün-yang, Szechwan) before the Double Ninth Festival (September 28). At Yün-an he fell ill and remained there until the spring of the next year.

V K'uei-chou

After lying sick at Yün-an hsien,
I am moving to the White Emperor's city.
Spring knows that the willows urge her to depart;
The river gives us clear water to sail.
I hear men talking of their farm work;
I see the birds' delight in the hills' brightness.
Yü's labors cleft the rocks in many places;
For a while we find land that's nearly level.

Moving to K'uei-chou[54]

Although at Yün-an Tu Fu was still expressing thoughts of returning home and still hoping for a post at court, he was to stay in K'uei-chou (modern Feng-chieh, Szechwan) for two years. K'uei-chou stood at the western entrance to the long Yangtse Gorges which extend downstream to I-ch'ang in Hupeh. It was again a new area for Tu Fu with distinctive scenery, manners, and customs, which in part may account for the very large numbers of poems he wrote in these two years: more than a quarter of his collection belongs to the K'uei-chou period. K'uei-chou was also a place of some historical associations. It had been the capital of Kung-sun Shu who had held Shu at the end of the former Han dynasty and had styled himself White Emperor. Thus Tu Fu often calls K'uei-chou "the White Emperor's city." There were temples to Liu Pei, ruler of the Three Kingdoms state of Shu, and his faithful minister, Chu-ko Liang.

Tu Fu and his family first set up house among the hills to the northwest of the city. Later, he himself stayed in the West Pavilion (*Hsi ko*), an official residence inside the city, which was the setting or the point of departure of a number of his famous poems, such as,

Night hues lengthen on the hill paths;
My high chamber is next the Water Gate.
Thin clouds at cliffs' edge sleep;
The lonely moon in the waves tosses.
Cranes follow each other in silence;
Wolves find their prey and howl.
I do not sleep for worry over war,
Yet have no strength to right the world.

Spending the Night in the Pavilion
by the River[55]

Tu Fu's quarters in the West Pavilion may have been due to the
kindness of Po Mao-lin, who came to K'uei-chou as prefect in the
late autumn of 766. In a note to one of his poems he states that
the prefect often shared his monthly salary with him. In return,
the poet no doubt acted as an unofficial secretary to the prefect.
It may well have been through Po Mao-lin's generosity that
Tu Fu in 767 became a man of some property. He had a house
and rice fields in East Village on the banks of the East Nang
Stream, which was on the eastern side of K'uei-chou, and a second
house with orchards in Nang-hsi, west of the Nang Stream to the
west of the city. His poems show him moving between the two.

With so many poems dating from these years a high proportion were, of course, still poems written for immediate occasions.
At the same time, this was a great period of recollection and
reminiscence in his life. Without K'uei-chou very little would be
known of his early years before his own poetic record begins. In
K'uei-chou, too, he wrote many of his "set-piece" works: the eight
"in memoriam" poems, the *lü-shih* series *Generals*, *Autumn
Thoughts*, and *Feelings on Ancient Sites*, in which he displays the
final perfection of his technique.[56] An outstanding characteristic
of Tu Fu's genius was his ability to sustain and refine his creative
energies virtually to the end of his life. His death in 770 can be
called a loss in much more than the usual conventional sense, for
his energies were still unspent.

Although with his farmland and orchards his life was more
secure in 767 than at most times in his later years and his health
was generally better, by the autumn he was thinking once more
of returning home, perhaps indeed because his health was better.
One of his brothers, Tu Kuan, had visited him during the summer
and had returned to Lan-t'ien, near Ch'ang-an, to fetch his bride.

He was apparently planning to settle in the south. In one of two poems Tu Fu addressed to him, he suggests that they may meet at Tang-yang (Hupeh) on Wang Ts'an's famous tower.

> At the Ch'u pass it was hard to part;
> In Lan-t'ien do not be delayed!
> Your clothes will be exposed to white rime;
> Your saddle horse will endure the chill autumn.
> When the full gorges are piled with Kiang water,
> I'll unfurl my sail on an eighth month boat.
> If on this occasion we get drunk together,
> It will have to be on Chung-hsüan's tower.[57]

The "eighth month boat" was not taken, but eventually another poem declared his intention to start in the middle of the first month of the new Chinese year (some time after February 3, 768), and this time he fulfilled his intention without very much delay. In spite of his very great poetic activity in K'uei-chou, he left it without any deep expression of regret. He had become perhaps inured to leaving places.

> Mosses and bamboos I have always been fond of,
> But like duckweed and thistledown I have no fixed place.
> In distant travels my children have grown tall;
> In many places I have left groves and houses. . . .[58]

VI   *Last Years*

The last three years of Tu Fu's life were spent appropriately enough, since wandering had steadily become the grand theme of that life, in travels within the area which forms the modern provinces of Hupeh and Hunan. His first place of sojourn was Chiang-ling, where he stayed until the autumn of 768. He found old friends in Chiang-ling and they might explain his lingering there. If he had thoughts of going to Ch'ang-an, these would have been checked by the news of a fresh Tibetan invasion in the northwest in the late autumn. In fact, he went next to Kung-an, about thirty miles south of Chiang-ling.

In Kung-an one of these notable encounters which bridge different generations occurred, for he met and wrote a poem for Li Chin-su, the father of the remarkable and short-lived poet of the early ninth century, Li Ho (791–817). Tu Fu and his family stayed in Kung-an for some two months, but before the end of the

Chinese year they were on the move again to Yüeh-chou on the northeastern shores of the great Tung-t'ing Lake.

> In the north city the watchman's stick again is about to stop
>   sounding;
> The morning star in the east also does not delay.
> The neighbors' cocks' country cries are just as yesterday:
> These appearances and activities, how long can they continue?
> Our boat will steer imperceptibly away from here;
> On rivers and lakes we shall go far with no destination.
> Once out of the gate, in a twinkling our tracks will be old,
> But medicines will be with me wherever I go.
>
> *Starting from Kung-an at Dawn*[59]

If the traveler's course was uncertain, the poet's sympathy for suffering was as strong as ever. In Yüeh-chou he wrote what some critics acclaim as the greatest poem of his late years, *The Year is Ending*.

> The year draws to its close with many north winds;
> The Hsiao and Hsiang and Tung-t'ing lie amid white snow.
> The fishermen's nets are frozen in the winter's cold;
> While the Mo-yu shoot wild geese with twanging mulberry bows.
> Last year the high price of rice made the army go short;
> This year the low price does great hurt to the farmers.
> The high official on his big horse is sated with wine and meat,
> While these people's shuttles are empty of thread in their straw
>   huts.
> The men of Ch'u prize fish and don't prize fowl;
> Don't uselessly kill the south-flying geese.
> Worse, I hear everywhere sons and daughters are sold;
> Kindness is cut off and love repressed to pay taxes.
> In the past men were seized for private minting;
> Now it is permitted to mix lead and iron with bronze.
> If one made money by carving mud, it would be very easy to get!
> But true and false ought not to mingle for so long.
> On every city wall painted war bugles are blown;
> When will there be an end to the plaintiveness of such tunes?[60]

The early months of 769 went by in sailing across the Tung-t'ing Lake and up the Hsiang River, with sightseeing, parties, and always poems, until he reached Heng-chou (modern Heng-yang, Hunan). Now he was going south away from home.

Spring banks to peach blossom waters;
Cloudy sail amid a maple tree wood.
Stealing my life, I am ever moving away;
Going farther from home, my tears fall faster.
Every day that, old and sick, I travel south,
My ruler's favor draws my heart to the north.
All my life, my songs have been inevitably sad,
But I have never found anyone to understand them.

Travelling South[61]

From Heng-chou he went north again to T'an-chou (modern Ch'ang-sha, Hunan), where he stayed through the winter of 769 and the spring of 770.

In the prefectures and kingdoms of the empire up to the
      Great Wall
There is not one city without armor and weapons.
How can we cast the armor into farm implements
That oxen may plow every inch of the abandoned fields?
When oxen finish plowing, the silkworms will be ready.
We shall not weary brave soldiers with streaming tears.
Men will harvest, women spin, and once more go singing.

Silkworms and Grain [62]

The hope of *Silkworms and Grain*, generally regarded as a T'an-chou poem, was too visionary for the time. Even in his last months he was driven out of T'an-chou by a local military revolt of the kind with which he had become so familiar. When he managed to return, and, in the late autumn of 770, was thinking once more to set out for Ch'ang-an, news may have reached him that the Tibetans were once more on the march toward the capital. He died in the winter.[63]

Tu Fu wrote his last poem—a long poem of seventy-two lines—while lying ill in his boat on the Tung-t'ing Lake; it is elaborate, allusive, passionate, full of homesickness and anxieties for himself, his family, and his country.

CHAPTER 4

Tu Fu and Poetry

> A name, how should my writing make?
> Office must be in age and sickness quit.
>
> *Thoughts of a Night Traveler*[1]

THIS ANTITHESIS of literature and official service was a crux about which Tu Fu's thoughts played in his last reflective years. As he came in the years of "age and sickness" to sum up his life and its achievement, he faced the dilemma, presented to all creative writers by traditional Chinese society, which, for all that it was a highly literary society and honored literary success, gave no independent status to the man of letters. The acquisition of education—the ability to read and write the difficult Chinese script and a knowledge of ancient books written in it— gave a man entry into the governing bureaucracy and a sense that official service was the only proper path for his career. To serve the emperor and his people was the one profession theoretically open to the possessor of a literary education. The theory of the state and the society did not permit a man who discovered political talents in himself to adopt the profession of poet. Yet, when Tu Fu looked back over his life, he could not but realize that for a great part of it he had followed the occupation of poet. That he did recognize it and was prepared sometimes to state it can be shown from his poems. For example, the often quoted line from the poem *Tsung-wu's Birthday*:[2] "Poetry is our family's business," apart from showing respect for his grandfather, certainly indicates that he saw himself especially as a poet. In the poem[3] he wrote commending two poems of Yüan Chieh, he states more directly:

> I belong to the class of poets
> And have gained a wide repute in the world.

Yet the gnawing anxiety of the insoluble conflict of theory and fact remained for him and intruded again and again. He never smoothed his difficulties to the point where he could take his stand without any equivocation. His views on poetry and his own practice of it are expressed as *obiter dicta,* as "random thoughts," even where they occupy whole poems.

The longest such expression is in *Chance Topic* (767),[4] which has been described as Tu Fu's "own preface" to his poetry.[5] This is a poem of many shifts and turns and many references. It will be best to translate it in sections with comment and explanation interspersed.

> Literature is a matter of a thousand ages;
> Its success is known in one's heart.
> Writers all stand in different ranks,
> But fame is surely no random favor.
> The *Sao* poet was, alas, no more,
> When the way of Han flourished.
> The early writers made the first soaring;
> The late writers embellished the work.
> Good writers of later times all had ancient examples,
> But from each generation there are fine models.

The "*Sao* poet" is Ch'ü Yüan (fl. ca. 300 B.C.), the supposed author of the early pieces in the anthology *Ch'u-tz'u,* which provide an ancestry for the long descriptive *fu-poem,* developed during the Former Han period (second and first centuries B.C.). In view of Tu Fu's many references to the Former Han *fu* writers, it seems likely that he again has them in mind with "the way of Han" rather than the five-word *shih,* which traditionally began with Li Ling and Su Wu in the first century B.C. The next two lines are understood to refer to the *shih* poets of the period between Han and T'ang (third to sixth centuries). Some then take "good writers of later times" to indicate Tu Fu's immediate predecessors in the T'ang period. Whether or not the lines need to be read so specifically, Tu Fu was certainly insisting, in a manner repeated in many prefaces to Chinese literary collections, on a continuing tradition of literature from antiquity ("literature is a matter of a thousand ages"). He turns in the next section to his own relation to the tradition and the models it offered.

> My principles are those of the Confucian school;
> My mind has been exercised from my youth.
> Long have I cherished the Southern Dynasties' excellences;
> I have declined with deep regret the rarities of Yeh.
> The coursers were all noble steeds;
> The unicorn had splendid offspring.
> My "cart-wheel" has been vainly hewn;
> To "roof my hall" the will still is lacking;
> Idly I have composed a "Hermit's Discourses";
> To no end handed down a "Young Wife's Memorial."

The emphasis of the first two lines, which are not very clear, is probably upon study. Of this Tu Fu makes great point elsewhere, claiming in a much quoted line to have "worn out ten thousand rolls" (books).[6] The poets of the Southern Dynasties, Hsieh Ling-yün (385–433), Hsieh T'iao (464–94), and still more Yü Hsin (513–81) and his contemporaries exercised an important influence on Tu Fu's diction. The role of T'ao Yüan-ming (365–427) was to be for Tu Fu, whenever he took up his hermit stance, a kind of alter ego. Thus the "borrowings" from T'ao Yüan-ming are particularly deliberate. Yeh was the capital of the Three Kingdoms state of Wei, where Ts'ao Ts'ao (155–220; "the unicorn") and his sons ("the splendid offspring") Ts'ao P'ei (186–226) and Ts'ao Chih (192–232) created a literary court for men like the "Seven Masters of Chien-an" (K'ung Jung, Ch'en Lin, Wang Ts'an, Hsü Kan, Juan Yü, Ying Ch'ang, and Liu Chen; "the coursers"). Although Tu Fu on occasion compares his ability to that of Ts'ao Chih, there is no conspicuous influence of the Wei poets on his work.

From his models he moves to lamenting the isolation of his own position through the figures of the wheelwright who cannot pass on his craft and of the father whose son does not continue his work. The "Hermit's Discourses" (*Ch'ien-fu lun*) is a work by Wang Fu (ca. 76–157), in which the title was intended to conceal the author's identity, while "Young Wife's Memorial" refers to a cryptogram devised by the scholar Ts'ai Yung (132–92). The implication of the references is that he does not expect his work to be understood, but he presumably also hints that like the *Ch'ien-fu lun* it is critical of the times.

The third section of the poem deals with his immediate situation, and here the poet's dilemma appears.

> I follow my feelings to alleviate my wanderings,
> As, burdened with sickness, I frequently move on.
> I am ashamed to have no plan for my country,
> And to seek only "a single branch to rest on."
> Amid the dust I am neighbor to wasps and scorpions;
> In the river gorges I am surrounded by dragons.
> Melancholy is the remoteness of the time of Yao and Shun;
> Continuous are the Ch'u-Han time dangers.
> The divine court has been annexed by rebels;
> Here the strange customs are also noisy and vulgar.
> Numerous are the star-bright swords;
> Dark are the "cloud and rain" pools.

He admits that much of his poetry is purely personal, written to unburden his individual distress and offering no solution for the great problems of the country. He returned to this thought in his last poem before he died, though there he expressed it indirectly, comparing himself to Yü Hsin, who composed his masterpiece *Lament for the South* as an exile in the north, and declaring he was unlike Ch'en Lin, whose memorials won the approval of Ts'ao Ts'ao.[7] The remoteness and barbarity of K'uei-chou, where he was staying, the protracted nature of the rebellions, which he compares to the time when the founder of Han was struggling to establish his dynasty ("the Ch'u-Han time dangers") are introduced as a sort of defense. For in such a time many good men ("star-bright swords") hide away and do not emerge (as the dragons in "the 'cloud and rain' pools" do not). The enormous disorder of the world grips his mind and he continues:

> In the two capitals headquarters have been set up;
> Over the whole world war banners are planted.
> The people of the southern sea have destroyed the bronze pillar;
> The people of the eastern air flee before the Tibetans.
> I hate the crows and magpies for bringing no news;
> I hate the bears for the fierceness of their growls.
> Sowing and reaping interrupt my poetry;
> In my humble abode I imitate the local customs.

The "two capitals" here are not Ch'ang-an and Lo-yang, but Ch'eng-tu and Chiang-ling, the headquarters of governors-general. The "bronze pillars" signifying Chinese authority were erected by Ma Yüan (14 B.C.–49 A.D.), conqueror of Nan-Yüeh (Kwangtung, northern North Vietnam).

It is clear that Tu Fu could not quite break free of the Confucian equation of literature (of which he did not regard poetry as
a separable part) with public service. Although he was very concerned in his late years with what sort of name he would leave to
the future and with the endurance of that name, it was always the
present use and effect of his writing that formed the subject of
his anxieties. He could not foresee that the future would call him
"poet-historian" and " poet-sage." Since by the standard he applied to himself he could only adjudge himself "a failure," he
ends this poem not with a conclusion, but with a dying fall of
reverie, letting his mind wander back to his beloved Ch'ang-an.

> I daydream of the White Pavilion in the old hills;
> I recall the autumn waters of the Imperial Lakes;
> But I dare not seek after beautiful lines;
> When melancholy comes, I write of separation.

When one considers that the remarkably productive K'uei-chou
period contains many of his most elaborate and most obviously
studied poems, the remark "I dare not seek after beautiful lines"
seems disingenuous. If Tu Fu did not "seek beautiful lines," who
ever did? He had, in fact, used the same phrase in self-reproach
earlier at Ch'eng-tu.

> A man of limited capacity, I was addicted to beautiful lines;
> Lest my words failed to startle I would strive until death.
> Now I have aged, my poems are all spontaneous;
> When spring comes, no flowers and birds deeply grieve.
> The newly added water fence serves to fish from;
> The formerly placed floating raft acts as a boarding stage.
> Where can I find poets with thoughts like T'ao's and Hsieh's,
> And make them write and make excursions with me?[8]

(T'ao is T'ao Yüan-ming; Hsieh is Hsieh Ling-yün.) This poem is
entitled *On the River Encountering Waters Like the Sea, I Wrote
a Short Poem on the Spot.* In view of the title one might argue
this is very much the feeling of a moment and one ought not to
take it as an important pronouncement on his attitude to poetry.
Since Tu Fu represents almost all his statements about poetry as
random remarks, this course is hardly open to the critic. This
short poem, however rapidly it was finally set down, surely has a
lot of thinking behind it. The idea in the fourth line of the poet

forcing his emotions on nature is not perhaps one which occurs in a flash of enlightenment.

Yet if this poem is set against other declarations, apparent inconsistency results. For example,

> I have molded my nature and intelligence to this thing:
> When I have finished polishing a new poem, I intone it to myself.
> I have made myself thoroughly familiar with the Two Hsiehs to
> share their skill;
> I have greatly imitated Yin and Ho in their intense care.

To Dispel My Grief VII[9]

The Two Hsiehs are probably Hsieh Ling-yün and Hsieh T'iao; Yin and Ho are Yin K'eng and Ho Sun, poets of the sixth century. This too is a poem from the K'uei-chou period. If an explanation is to be offered, the answer may be a psychological rather than a technical one. He cannot be saying "Once my poems were strenuously contrived; now I propose to write simply according to my feelings." He seems to be describing, in his eschewal of "beautiful lines," his attitude to poetry.

Account must be taken of the strongly social nature of Chinese verse. Tu Fu in his youth had pursued literature first of all as a means to a career. As a young man and as a middle-aged man he had lived in a metropolitan society where the writing of poetry and the exchange of poems were an accepted convention. That he should "startle by beautiful lines" was indeed a necessity. Up to the time when he left Hua-chou, the great majority of his poems can be described as "public" in the sense that they were addressed to a larger or smaller audience and were written in response to particular stimuli provided by that audience. While this still remains the case with a great many of the poems written in the last decade of his life, there are also many poems which are "public" only in the sense that they were written for publication, for no poet writes for his own eye alone. Their themes were determined by a personal choice and were less dependent on some external context. Poetry became the central preoccupation of his life, and he became more nearly a professional poet. His own consciousness of his altered situation may be the explanation of apparently contradictory remarks. "Spontaneous" would thus apply to the choice of theme, not to the manner of its treatment. A changed attitude to the place of poetry in his life may explain the increase in the tempo and extent of experimentation in his late poems and to some degree accounts for the very great range of his poetry, which was such that he could boast: "In poetry I have exhausted human topics."[10]

In his scattered remarks on poetry Tu Fu did not deliver himself of a generalization on the nature and function of poetry that would be likely to find inclusion in any universal dictionary of quotations. Perhaps he felt poetry to be too normal and natural an activity to single out it or its practitioners for special definition. Throughout, he emphasized study and intense application, succinctly summing up his position in the quatrain quoted above. Modern Chinese writers on Tu Fu with some knowledge of Western ideas of the poetic process, however, cannot fail to draw attention to his frequent use of the word *shen* ("spirit") and to equate it with the concept of inspiration. Such an equation across a wide cultural and linguistic divide is likely to be imperfect, since the associations and extensions of such an abstraction are almost bound to differ. In fact, Tu Fu nowhere talks about the abstraction "inspiration" but uses *shen* in phrases such as *ju yu shen* ("as if there were a spirit") for descriptive purposes. In such cases he is describing poetic excellence and there will be no harm in the rendering "inspired," since the connotation of the English word is likely now to extend little further than excellence. But his examples may be considered. The earliest is in the *Twenty-two Rhymes* to Wei Chi.[11]

> In reading I wore out ten thousand rolls;
> In plying my brush I was as inspired. (*ju yu shen*)

Here certainly Tu Fu uses the figure as a definition of his own literary skill. The use of the double negative form of the phrase in *Thirty Rhymes to Hermit Chang Piao* (759) is similar.

> Your "draft-style" calligraphy, how archaic!
> Your poetry is never not inspired![12] (*pu wu shen*)

When a third example (761) is considered, the definition, so long as one assumes that the poet's standpoint has remained constant, seems to become sharper, because here he is using a well-known allusion.

By the country temple river and sky spread out;
By the mountain door flowers and bamboos have secret beauty.
A poem would need to have a spirit's aid;
I have had the luck to make a visit in spring.
The rocks by the path wind about me;
The clouds over the stream of themselves move and stay.
In the monastery boughs all the birds are roosting;
A wanderer, at sunset I return to sadness.[13]

The third line in context (it is usually quoted without) is a particular not a general statement. It refers to the story of how Hsieh Ling-yün achieved his line "the pool bank grows spring flowers" through the appearance of his dead cousin Hsieh Hui-lien in a dream. "In these words there was a spirit's aid," he is reported to have said. [14] To interpret, what Tu Fu is saying is that to capture the scene before him (which, of course, he does), some supernatural aid is needed or one would need to be "inspired." This is after all only an oblique way of expressing the beauty of the scene and thus like the previous two examples reduces to a form for the superlative.

In the rather strange *Achieving a Poem While Drinking Alone* (757), the same underlying reference is present, but is turned in a slightly different direction.

The lamp flower, how fortunate!
The wine's green just happens to be at hand.
In drunkenness I can bear to be a stranger;
For the poem to be finished I feel there was a spirit.
Swords and lances are still before our eyes;
How can my Confucian learning provide for me?
I am wretchedly constrained by my petty office,
And bow my head in shame before the peasants.[15]

(The form of the charred wick of a lamp, called its "flower," was interpreted as an omen.) The fourth line, which, incidentally, can be very misleading, if cited out of context, stresses that he does not understand how he managed to write the poem; it is not self-congratulation on its excellence. This in fact keeps very close to the original sense of the allusion. To translate *yu shen* here as "inspired" would probably give a false impression.

These examples hardly demonstrate that Tu Fu had formulated a concept of "inspiration" as an additional necessary part of a poet's equipment beside intense application. All this is not to say he discounted the place of genius. He would have called it "talent" (*ts'ai*), and it would have been for him a basic assumption.

It is perhaps a little disappointing that Tu Fu who wrote so much poetry and who became for some later schools of Chinese poets virtually the god of poetry should have produced so little by way of definition or precept. What little he did offer was often pointedly labeled "random thoughts" and was mostly set in the shortest of all forms, the four-line *chüeh-chü*. *Chance Topic* is a fortunate exception.This use of the *chüeh-chü* for pronouncements on literature, which later writers often followed, was perhaps not one of Tu Fu's happier contributions to Chinese traditions. Generally lacking opportunities for external reference and comparison (apart from Buddhist Sanskrit), literary criticism in premodern China had considerable problems of terminology and definition, which were not helped by the use of the extremely terse *chüeh-chü* form.

Tu Fu's prototype for later *lun-shih chüeh-chü* ("Quatrains on Poetry") was his series *Six Quatrains Composed in Jest*.[16] These were clearly written as a polemic against some current attitudes to writers of the past. In the late seventh century a reaction, generally associated with the name of Ch'en Tzu-ang (656–95), had begun against the elaborate diction of the "Ch'i-Liang" style of Yü Hsin and the poets of the sixth century (Ch'i and Liang were two of the Southern Dynasties). In the *Six Quatrains* Tu Fu rallies to the defense of Yü Hsin and of the "Four Heroes of Early T'ang," Wang P'o, Yang Ch'iung, Lu Chao-lin, and Lo Pin-wang. These four poets were contemporaries of Ch'en Tzu-ang but were regarded as followers of Ch'i-Liang.

Although the *Six Quatrains* have attracted a good deal of attention, both because they contain internal problems of understanding and also because they are a rare document in the history of Chinese criticism, their essential message is a fairly simple counsel against partisan attitudes. "Let us not despise the men of today, let us love the ancients." This was in keeping with Tu Fu's catholic approach in both subject and treatment. He was unwilling to reject any model which he felt appropriate to any particular purpose. His catholicity kept him apart from attempts to reject "Ch'i-Liang" and return to "Han-Wei."

CHAPTER 5

The Forms of Tu Fu's Poetry

SINCE TU FU is by universal consent the master technician of T'ang poetry, one would expect him to have used the various poetical forms available to him with discrimination and deliberate purpose. A general review of his collection according to its forms should thus afford some preliminary insights into his aims and achievements.

By the High-T'ang period (so named from its embracing the lives of Tu Fu, Li Po, Wang Wei, and others of the greatest names in T'ang poetry) all the forms of *shih* were complete. They fall into two major divisions, distinguished as the "old forms" (*ku-t'i*) and the "new forms" (*chin-t'i*) or *lü-shih* ("regulated *shih*"). Both forms used the two basic *shih* meters of respectively five or seven words[1] to each line with end rhymes in the even lines of the poem. The old forms continued essentially unchanged from the period preceding T'ang, that is, without restriction upon the tones of the words used, the end rhymes, the number of lines to a poem, and without obligatory parallelism in construction.

The "new forms" had grown up through the introduction of limiting features into the old forms and their gradual crystallization over a long period spanning the fifth to the seventh centuries. Their final forms required the maintaining of a pattern of contrasted level (*p'ing*) and oblique (*tse;* the rising, falling and abrupt) tones, thus limiting the freedom of choice of words within the line, since most words had one fixed tone. This tonal restriction applied also to the rhyme words. Further, in two of the three "regulated forms" the number of lines in the poem was restricted, the *lü-shih* proper to eight lines and the "cut-short" (*chüeh-chü*) to four. The extended *lü-shih*, the *p'ai-lü*, was in fact a poem composed entirely of parallel couplets to any number from five onwards according to the poet's choice. In the *lü-shih* proper the second and third of the four couplets were of parallel construction. The *chüeh-chü* was half of a *lü-shih*, cut, as it were, in different ways. It could be completely without parallelism, thus corresponding to the first and last couplets of the *lü-shih;* it could have parallel construction throughout, thus corresponding to the middle couplets of the *lü-shih;* it could have parallelism in either the first or the second couplet, thus corresponding to either the second or the first half of the *lü-shih*.

There were thus four forms, each with a five- or seven-word meter variant (called in Chinese *wu-ku, ch'i-ku, wu-lü,* etc.; i.e., five-word old form, seven-word old form, five-word *lü-shih*, etc.), available for the poet's choice. The nature of Tu Fu's choice and individual use of these forms can now be examined.

A simple numerical count of Tu Fu's poems and their distribution among the various forms tends to be rather misleading. Chinese generally count as separate poems all pieces whether they have individual titles or are items in a series with a collective title. A count on this basis will give a grand total of over 1,450 poems (the actual figure varies slightly according to the inclusion or exclusion of a small number of poems of doubtful authenticity); to count only titles would reduce this figure by about a quarter. This kind of simple count will show that more than half of Tu Fu's poems are five-word (621) or seven-word (151) *lü-shih*, and that while there are thirty-one five-word *chüeh-chü*, there are only four seven-word *p'ai-lü*.[2] Such figures will hide the fact that in volume, at any rate, the *lü-shih* do not make half the collection and that one of the *p'ai-lü* (actually a five-word, not a seven-word) is longer than the thirty-one five-word *chüeh-chü* together. But such statistics are, in any case, of very limited significance in the study of poetry.

I *The "Old Forms"*

The seven-word old form had, when it came into Tu Fu's hands, a tradition of being a popular ballad form, and hence of being a form to be used for adaptations of folk song or for works to which the poet desired to give a popular character. This was the natural form for Tu Fu to choose for his works on public issues, for ex-

ample, for his protest against the continuation of the policy of
military expansion in *Song of the War Carts*.[3] It was an even more
obvious form to use when writing of ordinary people, such as the
firewood-gathering women of K'uei-chou.

> The virgins of K'uei-chou are gray-haired;
> At forty and fifty they are still without husbands.
> Even less in times of disorder can they be married;
> All their lives, they are resentful and long sigh.
> Local custom makes men sit and women stand;
> Men keep the house while women go out.
> Eight or nine out of ten bear firewood home,
> And sell the firewood for the home's needs.
> Even to old age twin hair knots hang down their necks;
> With wild flowers and mountain leaves, fixed with silver pins.
> Taxing their strength they climb the steeps or gather at the
>   marketplace;
> They risk their lives for money at the salt wells also.
> Tear traces mingle with their makeup and head ornaments;
> For the land is narrow and cold, hemmed in by mountains.
> If one were to say the Wu Hills' women are ugly,
> How could Chao-chün's village be there in the north?

> *Song of the Firewood Carriers*[4]

A very high proportion of Tu Fu's one hundred and twenty-
eight seven-word old poems have some word for "song" in their
titles. This does not appear to have any technical significance.
Any T'ang *shih* could be sung; it required only that singers
should take it up and sing it. It seems that Tu Fu often used the
appellation "song" to indicate the ballad character of the poem,
but also to represent the depth or, in some cases, the exuberance
of the emotion he was seeking to convey. One would not at first
perhaps expect that Tu Fu would use this particular form for
personal topics. Yet while it is the case that many of his most
"public" poems, for example, the "Laments" written during his
captivity in Ch'ang-an in 756, are to be found in this form, personal poems do appear among the earliest examples. Of a poem
like *A Missive to the Gentlemen of Hsien and Hua* one could
perhaps say that it is a public appeal on his own behalf.

> The ranks of the capital officials are crowded with talent;
> With soft furs and swift horses they face the ice and snow.
> At Ch'ang-an's bitter cold whoever should grieve?

Yet the old rustic of Tu-ling's bones almost break.
The "Southern Hill bean shoots" have soon withered;
The "Blue Gate melon field" is newly cracked with frost.
The "country bumpkin" has grown "stiff-necked,"
While old court friends' civility is ended.
Of course I am rejected, being at odds with the times;
Still more when I am careless and clumsy in affairs.
I lie hungry continuously for almost ten days;
My worn robe surely has not just a hundred patches.
Sirs, don't you see in the desolate house at evening
This old man silently shedding tears of blood?[5]

This poem does contain a few fairly simple and well-known allusions. In general, Tu Fu properly avoided abstruse or cunningly wrought allusions in poems in this form, as clearly these would detract from its vigor and directness. Where the subject demanded it, he could achieve an authentic simplicity of language; in other cases, while the construction remained simple, the language might be exotic if the subject required this. *Song of Fair Women*[6] is an obvious example.

The *ch'i-ku* form is generally the vehicle of Tu Fu's most vigorous and impassioned poetry. His practice of introducing occasional lines of irregular length—sometimes very long lines of nine, ten or even eleven words—which are a feature of the early *yüeh-fu* ballads of the Han period, is clearly a device to secure a less measured tempo. Direct speech and the appeal to the audience ("Sir, don't you see") are common. Hyperbole which is generally widespread in Tu Fu's poetic diction reaches its extremes in the *ch'i-ku*. "Where can I find a mansion of a million rooms?" in *Song of My Thatched Roof Shattered by the Autumn Wind* is a famous example. Another powerful example is in *Song of the Ancient Cypress*, which may be quoted also as a specimen of the symbolic or allegorical poem for which Tu Fu fairly often used the *ch'i-ku* form. The symbolism in this poem is fortunately not too obscure; to a great extent it is internally explained. It is a K'uei-chou poem, usually dated 766. The cypress, standing in front of the temple of Chu-ko Liang (K'ung-ming; the Martial Marquis), faithful minister of Liu Pei, First Ruler of Shu, both symbolizes Chu-ko Liang, who was fortunate to find a ruler who could use him, and the unyielding scholar who is unlucky in his time and does not find employment. With the second he identifies himself. There is an ambiguity in the middle of the poem, where he does not make it clear, after his reminiscence of the similar temple at Ch'eng-tu, which temple and cypress he is describing. It is perhaps a case of either or both.

Before K'ung-ming's temple is an ancient cypress;
Its trunk like bronze, its roots like rocks.
From its frosted branches rain drips for forty spans;
Its dark hue mingles with the sky for two thousand feet.
Clouds come, vapor-linking it to the Wu Gorge's length;
The moon comes out to join it in cold to the Snow Mountains'
    white.
Prince and minister once came together in a timely meeting,
So that the tree is still the object of men's love.
I recall where the road winds east of the Brocade River pavilion,
The First Ruler and the Martial Marquis share a shrine:
Towering branches and trunks upon the ancient suburban moor;
Hidden are the paintings in the deserted buildings.
Though standing apart with firm hold, the cypress has its place,
Soaring solitary into the void, it faces many fierce winds.
Its support, in truth, has been the spirits' power;
Its straightness was first the Creator's work.
When a great house is tottering, it needs beams and rafters,
That ten thousand oxen will not pull, a mountain's weight.
Even before its elegance is revealed, the world is startled;
It does not decline to be cut, yet how can it be carried away?
How should its bitter heart escape the attack of ants?
Its fragrant leaves at any rate have sheltered the phoenix.
Men of principle, scholars in retirement, do not resentfully sigh!
From of old great timber has been hard to use.[7]

The seven-word old form has been considered before the five-word, because it is certainly something of a special form of Tu Fu. Anthologists tend to select extensively from the seven-word old poems. It was a form he readily took up at moments of high emotion, but its examples are distributed fairly evenly throughout his poetic career. By contrast, the five-word old form, which is represented in his collection about twice as frequently, carries from beginning to end the main poetical record of his own life. The autobiographical *The Wanderings of My Prime, Five Hundred Words to Express My Feelings When I Went from the Capital to Feng-hsien, The Journey North, P'eng-ya Road,* and other long poems of travel and reminiscence are, one may say, naturally written with this form. But he used it for a very great variety of subjects, including in fact some which one is liable to think more characteristic of the *ch'i-ku*. That he should have written the *san-li san-pieh* ("Three Officer, Three Parting") poems in the five-word form contradicts the generalization that *ch'i-ku* is for the popular and *wu-ku* for the intellectual. Tu Fu perhaps did have a deliberate purpose in using the *wu-ku* in this case: he may have been seeking to capture the effect and to recall to his audience the character of Han five-word *yüeh-fu* ballads of similar theme.

This series of six poems shows Tu Fu in his greatest simplicity of expression. More often in the five-word old form he went to the other pole of abstruse allusion and elaborately balanced construction. Yet he had a very great sense of fitting language. The flexibility which he developed through treating a wide range of topics enabled him in his long poems to change manner and language as he moved through differing aspects or episodes of his theme.

II   *The Regulated Forms: Lü-shih*

A similar situation exists in regard to Tu Fu's use of the five- and seven-word meters in the *lü-shih* proper as is found in the case of the "old forms." The five-word is very much more widely represented in his work, but the seven-word appears to some degree to have held a special place with him; at least his technical experiments are rather more prominent in the *ch'i-lü*. To a great extent this was due to the greater possibilities offered by the longer line. It is noticeable that quantitatively four-fifths of his *ch'i-lü* come from the last ten years of his life and that it is from these years that, with the exception of the two *Curving Stream* poems[8] of 758, his most admired examples come. While there are still many fine *wu-lü* from his late years, the most famous of all are those of 756–57, especially *Moonlit Night* and *Spring Yearning*.

In Tu Fu's time the *ch'i-lü* was very much less widely used than the *wu-lü*, and he was undoubtedly in every way in the vanguard of its development. It is in fact said that the number of his *ch'i-lü* exceeds the grand total of *ch'i-lü* by all other poets of Early-T'ang and his own High-T'ang period. A particular development was his introduction of the linked series, which is perhaps a special manifestation of his general tendency toward works of a greater compass. The most conspicuous examples of the linked series are the K'uei-chou works, *Generals, Autumn Thoughts,* and *Feelings on Ancient Sites. Autumn Thoughts* is not only the most closely knit of the three series, it is also generally regarded by Chinese critics as the supreme example of Tu Fu's technique in the *ch'i-lü* form. Its analysis may be preceded by a look at *Feelings on Ancient Sites,* since in that series the references have mainly already been seen in other poems. In all these series it is the vision of the poet himself which makes the links. In *Feelings on Ancient Sites* his viewpoint is simple, and where it shifts, in the dimension of time, it does so without the studied effect that one can seem to detect in *Autumn Thoughts.*

I

Set adrift at the time of the northeast's storm,
I wander in the lands and under the sky of the southwest.
In dwellings on the Three Gorges I linger for days and months;
With people in Five Streams' garb I share the cloudy hills.
The Tatar's service of the ruler in the end was unreliable;
The literary wanderer, grieving his times, still may not return.
Yü Hsin's whole life was utterly miserable,
But his late poetry moved the men of the south.

Tu Fu naturally identifies himself with Yü Hsin. His turning from Yü Hsin to Sung Yü in the second poem might possibly be due to Yü Hsin having lived at Chiang-ling, where, by one tradition, was the home of Sung Yü. The latter was by (questionable) tradition an early *fu*-writer of the third century B.C. and a native of the southern state of Ch'u. There are a number of allusions in the poem to works attributed to Sung Yü.

II

At leaf-fall, I have a deep awareness of Sung Yü's grief;
His spirit and his style are also my models.
I sadly look back over a thousand autumns, overwhelmed with
    tears;
I am lonely in a different age and not his contemporary.
In his old home among the Kiang's hills vainly his writings
    remain;
The deserted Terrace of the Clouds and Rain was surely not a
    fantasy.
Worst of all, the Ch'u palaces were utterly destroyed:
Boatmen point to sites, but still there are doubts.

There is a famous Sung Yü line lamenting the sadness of autumn. The "Terrace of the Clouds and Rain" is a reference to the *Kao-t'ang fu,* ascribed to Sung Yü, which is alleged to be a criticism of the ruler's fondness for women.

If Chiang-ling may possibly connect the first and second poems, in the third the location has returned to K'uei-chou. The subject is Wang Chao-chün (the "Radiant Concubine") who was one of the great beauties of Chinese tradition. A concubine of the Han emperor Yüan (reigned 48–33 B.C.), she was selected by the emperor (who had never seen her) on the basis of an unflattering portrait to be given in marriage to a Hsiung-nu ruler. Too late, the emperor discovered his error, and could only wreak his wrath upon the painter. Wang Chao-chün died in her northern exile, but traditionally her tomb remained always green.

III

Where the massed hills and myriad gullies run towards Ching-men,
Still is the village where the Radiant Concubine was born and grew up.
Once she left the Purple Terrace, on and on stretched the northern desert;
Only there remains a green mound, facing the sunset.
In the painting her spring-fair face was crudely seen;
With tinkling girdle pendants, her moonlit ghost vainly returns.
Over a thousand years foreign words have been composed for the *p'i-p'a*;
Clearly are her resentments told in the tunes.

In the two final poems, Chu-ko Liang once more engages Tu Fu's attention.

IV

The ruler of Shu came to the Three Gorges to spy out Wu;
He was also in the Yung-an Palace in the year of his death.
The kingfisher plumes can be imagined in the empty hills,
Though his jade hall is desolate inside a country temple.
In the cryptomerias of his ancient shrine water cranes nest;
Where at summer and winter festival village elders come.
The shrine of the Martial Marquis is forever its neighbor;
For the inseparable ruler and minister the sacrifices are in common.

(The ruins of Liu Pei's Yung-an Palace were at K'uei-chou.)

V

Chu-ko's great fame has been handed down to the world;
The honored minister's surviving portrait is austere and lofty.
Confined to a third of the empire, he contrived his plans;
Over all antiquity, a solitary bird in the clouds.
I Yin and Lü Shang seemed on a level with him,
But Hsiao Ho and Ts'ao Shen could not match his sureness in
    command.
Fate turned and the Han throne finally could not be restored;
Firm of resolve, he sacrificed his life in his military service.[9]

I Yin and Lü Shang aided respectively T'ang, the founder of
the Shang, and Wen, the founder of the Chou dynasty, to their
thrones. Hsiao Ho and Ts'ao Shen were advisers of the founder of
Han. Chu-ko Liang's state, Shu, claimed legitimacy of succession
to the Han against its rivals, Wei and Wu.

The first theme of this series—exile, the uncertainties of political
affairs, no matter how steadfast a true minister may be—and the
second consolatory theme which conveys that the sufferer's name
is saved by the endurance of his own writings, in the songs of
others or by men's lasting respect are not intricately interwoven
into a symmetrical pattern. In *Autumn Thoughts* a more distinct
pattern can be discerned by analysis, though one should obviously
beware of forming a picture of Tu Fu mechanically filling in a
framework which he had devised in advance. The eight poems
form a unity to a degree where their order cannot be shuffled.
The viewpoint shifts continuously but logically between K'uei-
chou and Ch'ang-an (place), between present and past (time),
and between yearning and recollection (emotion).

The introductory first poem is wholly descriptive of the K'uei-
chou present; only the fifth and sixth lines lead away from K'uei-
chou tenuously but brilliantly.

I

The white dew shrivels and harms the maple forest;
The Wu Mountains' Wu Gorge has a desolate air;
The waves in the river leap up to join the sky;
The clouds over the pass cast gloom down to the earth.
The massed chrysanthemums a second time loose tears for other
    days;
The solitary boat, a single bond for my longing for home.
Cutting winter clothes, everywhere go quick the knife and rule;

On White Emperor's city height rapid beats the evening washing
    stone.

The second poem takes up the evening scene from the last line
of the first and projects the view rapidly, through the device of
the far-shining stars, to Ch'ang-an and as rapidly brings it back
to K'uei-chou again.

II

In K'uei-fu's lonely city, as the setting sun slants,
Always with the Northern Dipper's aid, I gaze toward the capital.
Hearing the gibbons, I may in truth let fall "three-note" tears.
Bearing a commission, I cannot take an "eighth month raft."
The painting hung Department's censers are far from my sick-
    pillow;
The mountain tower's whitewashed parapets hide mournful pipes.
Look! the moon from the wistaria on the cliffs
Already shines on the rush flowers before the islands.

The expression "three-note" tears plays on the line of a local
song: "The gibbons give their three-note cry and I weep upon my
robe." The fourth line makes use of a legend about the famous
Han envoy to the west (central Asia), Chang Ch'ien, who followed the Yellow River to its source and found that he could go
thence on a raft to the Heavenly River (the Milky Way). Tu Fu
means that he has no office to take him to Ch'ang-an, and thus the
Department of State Affairs with its paintings of statesmen and
fragrant incense burners is remote from him.

From night-yearning for Ch'ang-an Tu Fu moves in his third
poem to daydreaming at K'uei-chou and by the use of historical
analogies for his own frustrated career returns to Ch'ang-an as the
scene of his successful contemporaries.

III

The thousand-families city's mountain ramparts are quiet in the
    morning rays;
All day in the riverside tower I sit amid the blue haze.
Fishermen who have been out two nights come drifting back;
The swallows of the cool autumn still fly to and fro.
K'uang Heng, from memorials of remonstrance, had slight honors;
Liu Hsiang, in transmitting the Classics, was far from his heart's
    desire.

The young men who were my fellow students are mostly in high
  positions;
By the Five Tombs their clothes are light and their horses sleek.

In the fourth poem he remains mentally in Ch'ang-an, but
makes clear in the final couplet that it is all reminiscent reverie.

IV

I have heard it said that Ch'ang-an is like a game of chess;
For the whole of my life the world's affairs have been intolerably
  sad.
The mansions of princes and marquises all have new owners;
The wearers of civil and military dress are unlike those of former
  times.
In the passes and hills, due north, gongs and drums beat;
By carriages and horses, headed west, dispatches are sped.
Fish and dragons are quiet in the autumn river's cold;
My daily life in the old capital is in my thoughts.

In the fifth poem he employs an almost similar technique to
that of the fourth, indicating by the seventh line that it is all
dreaming.

V

The P'eng-lai Palace faces the Southern Hills;
The Dew-receivers' bronze pillars stand up into the sky.
Away to the west, from the Jasper Pool descends the Queen
  Mother;
Coming from the east, a purple mist fills the Han-ku Pass.
Like clouds removing, the pheasant tail palace screens are opened;
Sun encircled, the dragon scales make known the divine
  countenance.
From a sleep by the great river I am startled by the year's lateness.
How many times at the blue-studded door shall I be numbered
  in the court company?

The dream quality of this fifth poem is enhanced, when one
realizes that the vision does not remain in one period of time.
P'eng-lai was a T'ang palace name, but the Dew-receivers were
figures of "immortals" with bowls in their hands, set up by the
superstitious Emperor Wu of Han (reigned 140–87 B.C.). There
is a tradition of the immortal Queen Mother of the West (Hsi
wang-mu) meeting with Wu of Han, but she was also earlier a
companion of the wandering Emperor Mu of Chou. The "purple

mist" of the fourth line, heralding the arrival of Lao-tzu from Lo-yang, must take one to the seventh century B.C.

In the sixth poem he returns again in imagination to Ch'ang-an, but creates an almost physical link by his thought of autumn weather enwrapping all the way between.

VI

From Ch'ü-t'ang Gorge's mouth to the Curving Stream's banks,
Ten thousand *li* of wind and mist, joined in white autumn.
By the Flower Calyx Tower's enclosed way passed the imperial
          presence;
Into the Lotus Flower Small Garden entered the border anxieties.
Round pearl blinds and decorated columns circled yellow cranes;
From gilded ropes and ivory masts arose white gulls.
I recall how lovely was that place of song and dance:
The land of Ch'in, from old the domain of emperors and kings.

The suggestion of history in the last line of the sixth poem gives him a bridge to the seventh, which he starts by recalling the Han origin of the K'un-ming Lake, west of Ch'ang-an. Emperor Wu had created this lake in 120 B.C. for the training of naval forces for his expeditions against Nan-Yüeh.

VII

The K'un-ming Lake's water was the work of Han times;
Emperor Wu's banners appear before my eyes.
The Weaving Girl's loom thread is vain in the moonlight;
The stone fishes' scales are stirring in the autumn wind.
Floating rush grains are deep cloud black;
Dew-chilled lotus pods, spilt powder red.
The pass reaches to the sky, a way only for birds;
Rivers and lakes fill the earth for an old fisherman.

The seventh poem ends with the hopelessness of his yearning. "Rivers and lakes" have become an obstacle instead of a means to the realization of his dream. Once they were a delight. The final poem recalls that delight, as he sees again with the eye of memory the Mei-pei Lake which he visited and had written of a number of times during his years in Ch'ang-an.

VIII

Between K'un-wu and Yü-su it's a winding road,
Where Purple Pavilion Peak's shadow goes down into Mei-pei.
There were grains of fragrant rice left after the parrots' pecking.

There was a branch on the green *wu-t'ung* where a phoenix had
    long rested.
Fair women picked up kingfisher feathers to give as spring gifts;
Immortal companions, sharing a boat, at evening still went on.
My colorful brush I once set to that scene;
Now my white head sadly gazes and bitterly droops.[10]

These eight poems show many notable examples of Tu Fu's
experiments in parallelism and they should to some extent be
apparent in the fairly literal translation given. There is perhaps
no need to labor a feature which finally cannot be completely
appreciated out of its original language.

III   *The Regulated Forms: Chüeh-chü*

The four line *chüeh-chü* in the five- and seven-word meters was
regarded as an especial triumph of T'ang poetry, so that anthologies were devoted solely to this form. While Tu Fu's contemporaries in High-T'ang have been praised for their brilliance in
either the five- or the seven-word version, or, in the case of Li Po,
in both, the verdict of Chinese critics of the past has generally
gone against Tu Fu, and they often declare that he should not be
taken as a model. One must remember that the exemplary aspect
was commonly uppermost in the mind of the traditional critic
and the anthologist, as they served an audience of would-be
poets. In recent times there have been a few attempts to rescue
the reputation of Tu Fu's *chüeh-chü* from a different standpoint,
but the list of his most popular poems would still not include many
of his *chüeh-chü*.

This form was indeed the least favored by the poet himself:
there are only thirty five-word and one hundred-odd seven-word
chüeh-chü. It is immediately observable that almost all his quatrains date from the last decade of his life, after his arrival in
Ch'eng-tu; the one noteworthy exception is the *ch'i-chüeh To
Li Po*[11] dating from their period together in 744–45. This could
be an accident of transmission, but if it is not, it may be possible
to hold that in the last period of his life, when he was most consciously the poet, experimentalist, and innovator, he could hardly
ignore the form made famous by his friends Li Po and Wang Wei.

It can be said that a *chüeh-chü* is half of a *lü-shih*, but its writing may require a different approach, even perhaps a different

personality in the poet. It may be natural to expect that Tu Fu, with the technique to sustain and the patience to polish poems of unusually great length, might find this shortest form, the least congenial to his temperament. The *chüeh-chü* requires not sustained effort or even intense feeling, but a quick turn of observation or feeling that will isolate a scene or emotion forever in the space of four lines. It is noticeable that the majority of Tu Fu's *chüeh-chü* are written in series. This is, of course, not peculiar to him. To write a series of quatrains on a common theme, where each adds something to a general effect, is a different and probably lesser achievement than the single quatrain which can be felt to be absolutely complete in itself.

A convenient example for consideration is the seven-poem series *Walking Alone Along the River Bank to View the Blossoms* from the spring of 761.

I

On the river, I am ceaselessly provoked by the blossoms;
With nowhere to complain, I am driven quite mad.
For my southern neighbor, my drinking companion,
Ten days has gone drinking and left his bed empty.

II

Massed flowers in riot make the banks frightening,
As I pace along, reeling, truly afraid of the spring.
Yet poetry and wine, still I can manage.
There's no need to worry for a white-headed man.

III

River deep and bamboos still, two or three houses;
In a flurry, the red flowers; shining, the white.
To make answer to spring I know there's a way:
I need good wine to speed my life's passing.

IV

I gaze to the suburb where blossoms fill the haze;
Hundred-Flowers' tall tower is even more attractive.
How can I have wine brought and golden cups set,
And call for girls to dance before embroidered mats?

V

Before Priest Huang's tomb to the east of the river,
Exhausted by spring, I lean in the breeze.
A mass of peach blossom has come out with no owner;
The deep reds are lovely, but so are the light.

VI

At Madam Huang the Fourth's, blossoms fill the paths:
A thousand, a myriad, force down the branches.
Sporting butterflies linger, continually dance.
Of course there are sweet orioles to sing in time.

VII

It's no desperate matter to view the blossoms;
Though I fear, once they are gone, old age may press hard.
The abounding sprays easily fall in profusion:
The tender leaves should take care that they open slowly.[12]

While this series is not especially tight-knit and individual quatrains can be omitted without irreparable damage to the unity
(this is true of all Tu Fu's *chüeh-chü* series), no single quatrain,
except perhaps the first, seems quite strong enough to stand by
itself. Nevertheless, the seven poems do add up to a satisfying
treatment of the theme "Spring disquiets an aging man," and it
has to be admitted that they have not been reduced quite to seven
stanzas of a single poem. Tu Fu has achieved a sufficient complete-
ness in each poem to maintain a sense of rapid transition throughout the series and so capture for the whole something of the suggestiveness that is the chief requisite of the *chüeh-chü form*. The
separateness of the poems is emphasized in purely technical terms
by the variation of the rhyme words and the constructional pat-
terns.

Chinese critics from century to century stressed the importance
of the thought not being wholly (explicitly) expressed, and nowhere did they feel their precept to be more binding than in the
chüeh-chü. Clearly the danger for Tu Fu with his ever growing
interest in verbal technique was that he should draw the reader's
attention to the expression rather than stimulate his mind to
wander after the *unexpressed*. The series *Random Feelings*, probably also written in the spring of 761, shows an even greater tendency to depart from the desired suggestiveness of the form.

I

With her own eyes she sees the stranger can't be roused from
    his grief,
Yet shameless Spring's beauty comes to the river pavilion.
After she has sent the flowers to open in great excitement,
She makes the orioles chatter at too great length.

II

With my own hand I planted these peaches and plums; they don't
 lack an owner.
The old rustic's walls are low, but still they are in his own.
It seems the spring wind can be a cheat;
It came in the night and blew off several sprays of blossom.

III

Well knowing my thatched study is very low and small,
The river swallows deliberately come often,
With mud in their beaks to bespot my lute and books,
And besides chase flying insects to bump against me.

IV

The second month's finished and the third comes.
Aging, how many times can I meet the spring?
Don't brood upon the infinite after death!
But finish the limited cups of life!

V

Heartbreaking, the river spring's almost ended.
Leaning on my thorn stick, I walk slowly to stand by the scented
 island.
Mad willow catkins fly away on the breeze;
Frivolous peach blossoms drift away on the stream.

VI

I am intolerably lazy and do not go out of the village;
I call the boy to close the wicker gate in the daylight.
Green moss and cloudy wine, quiet within the grove;
Blue water and spring wind, darkness over the distant countryside.

VII

Scattered on the path, the willow catkins spread a white carpet;
Dotting the stream, lotus leaves string green coins.
Among the bamboo shoots a pheasant chick that can't be seen;
On the sands ducklings sleeping by their mother.

VIII

The leaves of the soft mulberries, west of the hut, can be plucked;
The slender wheat of the river bank again raises its spears.
In a man's life how many times turns spring to summer?
I'll not let go the fragrant must's honey sweetness.

IX

Outside the door the willows are frail and slender,
Just like fifteen-year-old girls' waists.

Who can say, when morning comes, one does not notice them?
The wild wind has pulled off the longest branches.[13]

These are charming descriptive poems. The range of devices for expression is quite great: the personification of Spring (rarer in Chinese than Western verse); the conceit of Spring as a thief; the willow-young girl simile in the last poem with its mildly erotic undertones; the several colloquialisms and the opposite formalism of the seventh poem. Such poems as these can be seen to have an effect on the diction of *tz'u*-poetry, which began to develop in the ninth century. But they remain descriptive rather than evocative and can for this reason be said not to employ the *chüeh-chü* to its best purpose.

In case the argument is being pressed too hard against Tu Fu for the sake of making a point, some of his single *chüeh-chü* should be considered. *Secretary Wang Had Promised Money to Repair the Thatched Hut. Since It Had Not Arrived, I Sent a Small Reminder* (the title is nearly as long as the poem) is an example of sharp humor.

I am angry with Secretary Wang:
He has not sent money for the Thatched Hut.
Yesterday he bade me worry about the spring rains:
Could he have forgotten that's when the hut would leak?[14]

The Temple of the Martial Marquis shows Tu Fu's characteristic ability to respond to the atmosphere of history and to hear the voices of its ghosts. In the temple to Chu-ko Liang at K'uei-chou he recalls the great soldier before his last campaign from which he did not return.

The painting in the temple has faded away;
The plants and trees on its empty hill are tall.
Still one hears him taking leave of the Last Ruler;
No more to sleep at Nan-yang.[15]

The language of this poem is very simple and the movement of thought to reach Chu-ko Liang's home in the last line is skillful, so that a truly evocative effect is achieved here. The uncertainty of homecoming is made to suggest the poet's own situation also without any actual reference at all. If one immediately sets against this quatrain *Returning Geese*, which is directly about homesickness, this latter seems unsuccessful, because its whole expression is too explicit.

There comes east a ten-thousand *li* traveler;
Now disorder is put down, when will he go home?
Heartbreaking the geese in the city on the river,
High up, flying due north.[16]

The range of subject in Tu Fu's *chüeh-chü* is little less wide than in the totality of his collection. The general aspects of the poet's personality and the abiding concerns of his mind are exampled within them. A disproportionate number of his comparatively few remarks on poetry and poets occur in this form and have already been discussed. He may have welcomed the means afforded by the brevity and general character of the *chüeh-chü* to stress that such thoughts were lightly spoken. If one puts aside the argument of how Tu Fu should have used the form and limits the judgment of the actual results of his own particular use of it, the most pleasing examples will after all be among the quatrains on scenery and his response to it, such as are represented by the two series translated above. Another favorite example, usually quoted out of the series to which it belongs, is:

Two yellow orioles sing in the green willows;
A line of egrets climbs the blue sky.
The window holds the thousand autumns' snows of the Western
    Range;
At the gate lie the ten-thousand *li* boats from Eastern Wu.[17]

In this strongly visual description the opposition of the simple parallelism in the first two lines to the striking antithesis of the eternal snows of the mountains and the boats which traverse the length of the Yangtse seems to be labeled unmistakably "Tu Fu."

Twentieth-century left wing critics, however, are likely to commend the quatrains on scenery only where they contain colloquialisms, and luckily they often do, and so can be held to have popular connections. For such writers the most significant of Tu Fu's quatrains are those which treat social or political subjects. These are mainly to be found in the seven-word rather than the five-word form. An especially unusual example is the three-poem series of 765, described by a recent writer[18] as the "san-li san-pieh" of the *chüeh-chü.*

I

The previous year in Yü-chou the prefect was killed;
This year in K'ai-chou the prefect has been killed.

The bandit gangs, one after another, are worse than tigers and wolves;
When they devour men, will they leave the wives and children?

II

Twenty-one families came into Shu together;
Only one man remained to go out of Lo Valley.
When he spoke of his parting from his two daughters,
He turned his head and groaned toward the clouds of Ch'in.

III

Although the imperial guards are valiant,
Their savagery is much like that of Tibetans and Tatars.
I have heard that in the fighting on the Han River
There were many women among the imperial troops.[19]

The reference to "women" in the last line is a caustic reference to eunuch commanders of the imperial army. Here, though these poems are entitled simply *chüeh-chü* and are so classified in some editions divided according to form, Tu Fu has abandoned the tone pattern. He is thus experimenting with a kind of pre-tonal *chüeh-chü* and apparently aiming at a deliberate naturalness, so that the comparison with the "san-li san-pieh" is not inapt. The second of the three can be regarded as a success, but the other two seem, like the majority of the social and political quatrains, to stagger under too heavy a burden of subject matter and to fall rather flat.

In summary, it may be said that of the various forms which Tu Fu employed he made the least successful use of the *chüeh-chü* in that he made it serve no particularly distinctive purpose in his poetry. Many of the *chüeh-chü* treat the same topics as poems in other forms and too seldom offer clear evidence for the preference of the shorter form.

IV *The "Regulated Forms": P'ai-lü*

Although later it became natural to think of the *p'ai-lü* as being an extended *lü-shih*, this was probably not the course of its historical development. Since the *lü-shih* in general arose out of the gradual application of restriction to the "old forms," which had no regularity of length, *lü-shih* of unfixed length would have preceded the particular development of the eight-line *lü-shih* which rapidly became the standard form. In Tu Fu's day a comparatively free situation may still have existed, with the eight-line *lü-shih* only the most favored form. In fact, the *lü-shih* longer than eight lines became generally standardized to a length of twelve lines from the ninth century onwards. The term *p'ai-lü* itself probably did not come into currency for another four centuries. Further indication of the fluid situation still existing in Tu Fu's time appears in the fact that some of his poems which are formally classified as "*p'ai-lü*" are "imperfect."

For Tu Fu, then, the five-word *p'ai-lü* was in the nature of an alternate form to the five-word "old form" and he made extensive use of it. Of the seven-word form he has only a very few examples, either perfect or imperfect, and this form is generally very rare in T'ang poetry. Thus his *ch'i-p'ai* may be regarded as a minor formal experiment. The range of the one hundred and twenty odd *wu-p'ai* is wide both in subject and in diction. He used this form frequently in his "poem-dropping" period in Ch'ang-an and not unnaturally in such poems strove to display his erudition and the brilliance of his technique. But during his captivity under the rebels he showed that he could cast simple words into this form and express the deepest feelings. Thus he wrote for his son:

> Chi-tzu is a good boy.
> When he was learning to speak the year before last,
> He asked and knew the names of guests,
> And could recite my poems.
> In the disorder of the age I pity his smallness;
> In the family's poverty he depends on his mother's love.
> To go hand in hand at Lu-men cannot be;
> A letter tied to a wild goose's foot, I cannot expect.
> The world is full of armies' banners;
> Among hills and rivers war horns moan.
> If I can return and we do not lose one another,
> Dare I say the day of our reunion is late?[20]

Examples of such comparatively simple language are in a minority, since this is not a form which Tu Fu would have employed for works to which he sought to give a popular character, but it continued to be throughout a form to which he readily turned to treat subjects of deep emotion. His poem of mourning for his friends Cheng Ch'ien and Su Yü who both died in 764 is a fine example.

Which of my old friends loved me?
All my life, Cheng and Su.
The living and the dead will not meet again;
Ruin only lies before me.
What man of genius still exists?
Literature is swept away to be no more.
As I wandered over ten thousand *li*'s extent,
News of their deaths came in a single year:
One on a bright day in the Central Plain,
The other in clear autumn by the Great Sea.
One's "dark terrace" faces the Northern Dipper,
The other's way to the nether springs is far off in eastern Wu.
For his offense he was sent to T'ai-chou;
In the times' perils he lost his high principles.
The other moved his office to the rear of the palace;
When grain was dear, he died unknown.
How can my streaming grief reach them?
I am full of anger that such things should be....[21]

This poem continues on its antithetical path for another twenty-six lines. The *wu-p'ai* joins the *wu-ku* as the vehicle of Tu Fu's longest poems; it was used indeed for his greatest tour de force, a poem of "one hundred rhymes"—a hundred parallel couplets. If John Keats' dictum that long poems are necessary to demonstrate the great poet has force, Tu Fu passes the test with great ease. His last poem was a *p'ai-lü* of seventy-two lines.

CHAPTER 6

Some Themes in Tu Fu's Poetry

Some Themes in Tu Fu's Poetry

THE CHINESE, perhaps out of necessity, brought on by large numbers of people, places, documents and books, have for much of their known history been great arrangers and classifiers. Encyclopedic arrangement by categories probably first appeared in dictionaries of the language and thence developed into the selection of literary quotations under topical headings to produce the *lei-shu,* generally called "encyclopedias" by Western students of Chinese. Since Tu Fu left a large number of poems on a wide variety of topics, his collection can be treated as a sort of *lei-shu* in itself. Such an arrangement was followed in a Southern Sung edition of the works, probably first printed in the period 1195–1224.[1] In this the poems have been arranged under seventy-two (a "lucky" number) headings, including a final miscellaneous category for those poems which cannot be fitted under the preceding seventy-one. The categories were created on the basis of both subject and genre, which inevitably led to quite arbitrary decisions. Yet, however arbitrary this type of arrangement may prove to be, it does suggest one particular way of approaching a large collection like Tu Fu's, since the breaking up of the general chronological ordering may sometimes give a fresh vision.

Here it is not proposed to look at Tu Fu's whole work under seventy-two or any other number of heads but to discuss and illustrate a few of the themes of Tu Fu's poetry which seem significant for varying reasons.

I *Poems of Travel*

Tu Fu's references to himself as a traveler, both literally and metaphorically, are legion. The circumstances of his life which sent him wandering over so much of China were undoubtedly a factor in the continuing appeal of the poet and his works over the centuries. His poems stirred feelings of identification in later travelers and local pride in those whose localities he helped to make famous by his writing.

Many of these legion references to himself as a traveler are indeed concerned less directly with travel than with homesickness. Nostalgia is so common a feature of Chinese poetry that it can hardly serve as a distinctive line of analysis. In Tu Fu it is a continuing groundswell. One may presume that the poems he wrote during the years of his travels in "Wu and Yüeh," which were undertaken for pleasure, struck a happier note, but none of these have survived. The travels of his later years he felt were imposed upon him as a result of the rebellion, and he seems throughout to have been unwilling to put aside the thought that he was a traveler perforce. A note of complaint or sadness can almost always be heard in poems where travel is described. These later travels were often, of course, perilous in themselves or undertaken in dangerous circumstances. Even where physical dangers were absent, the journey was not attended with any great comfort for the poet, who was often a sick man.

Nevertheless, Tu Fu, with his keen observation and his emotions given an edge by a sense of danger, produced some remarkable poems of travel, in which his hardships are treated with irony, his companions are shown compassion, and the barriers of land, water, and weather are accorded appreciation and awe. The character of Tu Fu's travel poems can be recognized as forming part of the ancestry of the records of travel and excursion (*yu-chi*), which were soon to become one of the distinctive and successful genres of Chinese prose-writing. The *yu-chi* displayed the basic characteristics of Chinese landscape poetry: they blended scene (*ching*) with the writer's emotional response (*ch'ing*) to it. Pure description of scene without personal response would be regarded as a geographical rather than a literary work.

The list of Tu Fu's travel poems in the edition mentioned begins with the two long poems of 757, *The Journey North* and *P'eng-ya Road*.[2] Only part of each poem deals with travel, and the travel description of *The Journey North* is interrupted by digressions.

> Slowly I go along the paths between the fields;
> Smoke comes from but few and isolated houses.

Of those I meet, many are wounded;
They groan and again they bleed.
I look back to Feng-hsiang district,
Where banners flicker in the twilight.
Onward I climb the cold hill-folds;
Often I come to watering holes.
The outskirts of Pin-chou sink into the earth;
Through them the Ching River ripples.
The Fierce Tiger stands up before me,
Whose dark cliffs once were split by its roar.
Chrysanthemums droop this autumn's flowers,
But the rocks bear ancient carriage tracks.
The white clouds arouse an exhilaration;
Here retired pursuits could be enjoyed.
The mountain fruits are often very small;
They grow mixed among chestnut oaks.
Some are as red as cinnabar;
Some are as black as lacquer;
Moistened by the rain and dew,
Sweet and bitter, all come to fruit.
I think of life within the Peach Blossom Spring,
And sigh the more for the stupidity of my course.
From the slope I gaze toward Fu Mound,
Over the rise and fall of hill and valley.
While I have raced on to the river bank,
My servant is still among the last of the trees.
An owl hoots among the yellow mulberries;
Field rats bow from scattered holes.
In the depth of the night we cross a battlefield;
The cold moon shines on white bones.
At T'ung-kuan an army of a million
Lately was scattered—how suddenly!
Which brought half the people of Ch'in
To be destroyed and turn to ghosts.[3]

In the travel description of *P'eng-ya Road* the portrayal of
action holds the central place; the emotion is mainly suggested by
the dramatic detail of the action; the scene is very lightly and
impressionistically drawn. In contrast, in *The Journey North* the
action is quietly indicated and the emphasis goes to the atmosphere and to the emotion which is allowed, one might almost say,
to run unchecked. The atmosphere of war and violence is built

up steadily through the first dozen lines of the passage: the deserted countryside, the wounded, war banners, watering holes for army horses, even the tiger-shaped cliffs are animated to add to the violent air. Then the white clouds call the poet's mind to a sustained thought of hermitage into which the berries and acorns before his eyes are drawn to add color. From this apparent daydream (there is almost no time sense, though the journey must have occupied a number of days) he hastens forward, anxious to reach Fu-chou and his family (he gallops ahead of his servant). Night again and a battlefield recall the disastrous defeat of the previous year.

Neither of these poems, in spite of its title, could be called a pure travel poem, and indeed the discursive nature of so much of Tu Fu's poetry makes classification by topic a frustrating exercise. In many poems whose titles suggest that travel is their subject, it proves to be only a minor theme. An exception, however, is the series of poems which Tu Fu wrote during the journey in 759 from Ch'in-chou to T'ung-ku and on to Ch'eng-tu. This long journey carried out in a short period over strange and extremely difficult terrain powerfully engaged the poet's mind and moved him to commemorate it in a continuing series of immediate impressions. Read together, these poems may be seen as a poetical *yu-chi*. There are more than twenty poems in all. With the exception of the first, the following come from the second stage from T'ung-ku to Ch'eng-tu.

Ni-kung Mountain

In the morning we travel over black mud;
In the evening we are still amid black mud.
The mud is not all from one time;
Many men have labored to ram the earth here.
I do not fear the unendingness of the road;
Only it could be like drowning.
My white horse has become an iron black;
My small son has turned into an old man.
A miserable gibbon crossed but fell;
A dead deer whose strength failed.
I send word to those coming from the north,
That from here on they should not hurry.[4]

Tree-bark Range

The road to the west of Chestnut Pavilion
Still reminds one of Phoenix Village.
In the last month of winter I lead the children,
Through hardship toward the gate to Shu.
Southward we climb the Tree-bark Range.
Whose steepness is hard to describe.
Streams of sweat cover our bodies;
The great cold is turned to heat.
Distant peaks rise in support;
A thousand cliffs go tumbling down.
For the first time I know that beyond the Five Peaks
Are other mountains to be honored.
Upwards, it blocks out the Great Brightness;
Downwards, it splits apart the vast earth.
Again I hear tiger and leopard fighting;
Often I cower under the scenery's grimness.
High up is an abandoned railed way,
Smashed like a broken carriage.
Below are winter green forests;
Over the rocks run long roots.
The western cliffs are outstandingly beautiful;
Brilliant as though abounding in magic fungi;
Richly stored with a golden aura;
Pure, without trace of sand or soil.
I recall looking at pictures of the K'un-lun;
Now my eyes are struck by the reality of Hsüan-pu.
With this before me, where should I want to go?
I am silently wounded in my aging spirit.[5]

Flying Immortals Railed Way

From T'u-men the mountain way is narrow;
The tiny path climbs up a fine hair.
Men have laid planks over the clouds, railed the
    precipices,
Made steps in the rocks, constructed a firm way.
In ten thousand gullies slant thin woods;
Amid deep shade strips of rushing water.
The winter sun outside is pale;
The continuing wind inside howls angrily.
When we halt at the bottom of the valley,
Only then do we realize the heights we've crossed.
Travelers, coming and going, sit or lie in disorder,

For men and horses are alike exhausted.
Our floating life has its appointed lot:
Hunger or fullness cannot be avoided.
But with a sigh I say to my family:
"Why did I do what you wanted?"[6]

Dragon Gate Railed Way

The clear river descends from the Dragon Gate;
On the sheer walls there is not a foot of soil.
The continuing wind is borne on high waves,
Which have rolled on since remote antiquity.
The perilous way winds in the midst;
Seen from below, it hangs like a thread.
Oh! who bored into the slippery rocks?
From which the floating bridge is propped, as it spirals.
My eyes blur as though in a mass of falling blossom;
My head swims as though struck by driving rain.
My "hundred years," I dare not anticipate;
One fall and how should I get them?
I have often heard of the Ch'ü-t'ang passage;
And know well enough about crossing Ta-yü.
All the dangers I have experienced in my life
Must, I fear, be counted from this time.[7]

This travel series stands out in Tu Fu's collection as the happy result of a particular time; it was not repeated.

II   *Poems on Paintings*

It is a cliché of writers on the cultural history of China that the arts of poetry, calligraphy, and painting are intimately related. Probably what quite often provokes this statement is the painting or calligraphy roll with its "inscribed" poems (*t'i-hua shih*). The connection of poetry and painting is, of course, valid in a wider and in an abstract sense, summed up in the famous remark of Su Shih (1037–1101) on Wang Wei that there was painting in his poetry and poetry in his painting. For Chinese poetry is strongly visual, while Chinese painting relies greatly upon suggestion. But here, only the narrower aspect need be considered, since the beginning of the practice of writing poems against one's own or others' painting is attributed to Tu Fu.[8]

Some twenty of Tu Fu's poems are *t'i-hua shih*, or have paintings or painting as their subject. The description of paintings is

an incidental feature of other poems. He clearly had a respect
and affection for painters and a strong critical insight into their
work. His approach and treatment in this group of poems is very
varied, but one general characteristic is at once obvious. This is
the device of rapid transition between the representation and its
subject. In this he may be seen to have contributed to a technique widely developed in Late-T'ang *shih* and in the *tz'u* poetry
of Late-T'ang and the following Five Dynasties period of deliberate ambiguity between the real and the painted.

Tu Fu and his contemporaries demanded that a painting
should "come alive." His praise for the painter is often expressed
in the description of the astonishment or fear of the beholders.
Yet few of these poems, although the praise they express may be
generous, are simply appreciations of a painting, but are injected
with personal thoughts, as are Tu Fu's poems on all themes.

The most famous of his poems on paintings is *Song of Painting*:
Presented to General Ts'ao Pa, written at Ch'eng-tu. Though the
poem gives glimpses into the situation of painters at Hsüan-
tsung's court in the earlier period of his reign, its subject is not
general, as the title might imply. It is essentially a testimonial to
the life of an old painter fallen on hard times, offered in consolation to its subject.

The General is a descendant of Emperor Wu of Wei,
But now his family have become commoners and are poor.
Though the heroic conquests are a thing of the past,
The artistic spirit is still preserved.
In his study of calligraphy he first followed Madam Wei;
His only regret is not to have surpassed Right General Wang.
While painting, he "does not realize old age is coming on."
"Riches and honors are to me like floating clouds."
During K'ai-yüan he was constantly received by the Emperor,
And by his favor often entered the Southern Fragrance Hall.
To the faded features of the statesmen in the Mist-Soaring
Pavilion,
The General's brush brought living faces.
On the heads of noble ministers were "Promoted Worthy" hats;
At the waists of fierce Generals, great-feathered arrows.
The hair of the Dukes of Pao and O bristled;
Their heroic aspect was alive with love of battle.

The former Emperor's "heavenly horse," Jade-flower Dapple,
Whom a host of painters had differently depicted,
That day was led beneath the Vermilion Terrace;
Rearing before the Palace Gate, he raised a great wind.
The General was ordered to spread white silk;
He earnestly devoted his skill to the planning.
In an instant a true imperial "dragon" appeared;
At one stroke all horses of all ages were made of no account.
Jade-flower is *there* above the Emperor's throne!
Above the throne and in the courtyard—a towering likeness!
His Majesty smiled and pressed gold upon him;
The stud keepers and the Master of the Horse all sighed.
His pupil Han Kan had early mastered his skill;
He too could paint remarkable likeness of horses,
Kan only painted the flesh and did not paint the bone;
He did not mind if the coursers' spirit was lost.

The General's skill in painting is truly inspired;
He will paint the portrait too of any excellent man he meets.
Now when he is a wanderer in time of war,
He often paints ordinary travelers.
In his straits he has come to suffer the contempt of the vulgar,
For in the world no one is as poor as he.
Only let him consider that from of old famous men,
All their lives, were disappointed and constrained.[9]

Ts'ao Pa's equine paintings would have had an especial appeal
for Tu Fu who had a deep affection for the horse and frequently
used it for symbol and allegory. *Song of the Bay from the Imperial Stables* describes the real horse from a painting, but ends by
turning the poem into a lament for the times' decline.

I have heard the Emperor's horses run a thousand *li* a day;
The one in the painting would certainly do so;
How valiant and heroic in will and bearing!
With the swishing of his great tail a north wind rises.
His coat is dark and glossy, his ears are yellow;
In his eyes are reddish flames and their pupils are square.
Brave is his dragon nature, equal to all changes;
Imposing is his heavenly frame, majestically planted.
Formerly the Director of the Imperial Carriages, Chang
    Ching-shun
Inspected the broken colts and choose one for perfect excellence.
Then he ordered the head groom to care for it in the
    T'ien-yü stalls;

He separately reared the courser, loving its noble qualities.
At that time there were four hundred thousand horses,
But Chang lamented that the ability of all was inferior.
So of this alone he had a likeness painted for men of the time.
When one views it by one's seat, it remains still fresh.
After many years things perish and leave a vain image.
Alas! how shall those strong feet gallop?
Now there are surely no Yao-niao and Hua-liu;
Because the times lack a Wang Liang or Po Lo, they die and
    are no more.[10]

In Ch'eng-tu, Tu Fu made the acquaintance of another well-
known painter, Wei Yen, who, when he came to take leave of the
poet, painted a pair of horses on the wall of his Thatched Hut.

Lord Wei came to say goodbye, for he was going away.
He knew I admired his unequalled painting,
And in jest took a bald brush and stroked out a Hua-liu.
Suddenly I saw "unicorns" start from the eastern wall.
One is cropping the grass, the other is whinnying;
I sit and see a thousand *li* before their frosty hooves.
In the times' perils how can I make them real?
That they may be with me in life and death.[11]

The poem was presumably inscribed by the painting on the
wall and in the end proved less perishable than the painting.
None of the works which Tu Fu so graphically described have
survived. He was himself very conscious of the mortality of paintings, how their colors faded and how murals, when the roof fell
in, were slowly erased by wind and rain.

His Excellency Hsüeh's eleven cranes
Were all painted from Ch'ing-t'ien birds.
The colors long since have all but gone,
But faded, as they are, they are still unusual.
Set high or low in separate attitudes,
They are imposing like tall men.
Excellent is the range of their aspiration,
Not just when the colors were fresh.
They could fly ten thousand *li* without effort;
Traveling in a flock, majestically forceful;
Dignified, with the white phoenix' bearing,
They do not flock together with orioles.
Before the high hall was destroyed,
They always gave refreshment to the honored guests.

Exposed to sun and dew on the outside of the wall,
In the end, alas, wind and rain will destroy them.
Among the red clouds is a real bird,
Ashamed to drink at a muddy pond.
Indifferently, it goes where it will;
Unrestrained, who can tame it?

*Hsüeh Chi's Painted Cranes on the Outside of the
Wall of the T'ung-ch'üan Yamen*[12]

For all the fortunate associations of the crane, the bird on which those who achieved "immortality" might fly away out of the realms of men, it was the hawk, companion to the horse in the hunting field, that particularly attracted Tu Fu as a subject for poetry, either in painted representation or in reality. There were specialists in hawk paintings, just as for equine subjects. Tu Fu has poems on the work of two hawk-painting masters, Chiang Chiao and Feng Shao-cheng, or rather a copy of the latter's work.

Song of Chiang Lord of Ch'u's Painting a Horned Hawk

The Duke of Ch'u has painted a hawk; the hawk has a horn.
Its killing lust is terrible, that it would bring it to the
    dark North.
Those who look at it are anxious lest it break from the arm
    and fly;
Painting teachers cannot aimlessly imitate it.
This hawk's painted likeness is in Eastern Mien,
So that the true form is, alas, vainly caught.
The swallows and sparrows among the rafters should
    not fear;
It cannot attain the ninth heaven in the sky.[13]

The thought of this poem is that the painted bird, in spite of the wonderful realism of the representation, is, in Mien-chou, out of its normal northern habitat, so that the likeness is caught to no purpose. One must imagine that this emphasis reflects symbolically the poet's own nostalgia, just as in the previous poem about the painted cranes, the real bird introduced for contrast in the final lines is also a symbol for the poet. The poem *Yang Chien Also Shows Me a Twelve-leaf Screen Painted with Hawks* serves him as a vehicle for recalling the past, when Hsüan-tsung moved with his court in winter to the warm spring on Li-shan and at the same time for suggesting that he himself is still capable of employment.

In recent times Feng Shao-cheng
Was skilled in painting birds of prey.
His Excellency has shown me this painting,
Which has undoubtedly reproduced his style.
The various positions all show the bird's solitariness;
It is very clear that its thoughts have a goal.
Its speed matches a thousand *li* horse;
Its spirit equals a general of ten thousand.
I remember how when to the Li-shan palace
The Han-yüan guards were moved in winter,
In the cold weather there was a great archer's hunt;
Such birds as this were all of regal spirit;
On such occasions there were no common talents;
Perfect marksmen all employed their manhood.
The painted bird is of kindred form;
One who recognizes it will be very moved.
In time of war there are few leisure days,
And the real bird grows old on its crag.
Yet for its lord it can remove the cunning hare,
And luckily return to the armlet.[14]

It would have been very interesting to have viewed through
Tu Fu's eyes one of the landscape paintings of his friend Wang
Wei, the acknowledged master of the genre, but there are only
his descriptions of the works of lesser painters, ambitious though
these sometimes seem to have been.

In a hall there should not be maple trees growing;
And strange there, for mists to rise from rivers and hills.
I heard that you had painted a map of China,
But on impulse changed it to an immortal's view....[15]

The landscape screen of Liu, the police commissioner at Feng-
hsien, an otherwise unknown artist, is praised so extravagantly
that one wonders if Tu Fu allowed politeness to cloud judgment.
The equally generous praise of *Song Inscribed in Jest on Wang
Tsai's Landscape Painting* may have been more merited as Wang
Tsai was a recognized painter.

Ten days to paint one river;
Five days to paint one rock;
Skilled work does not admit hurrying;
Wang Tsai will for the first time leave a true likeness.
Grand is the painting of the K'un-lun and Fang-hu,
Which will hang on the white wall of the high hall.

From Tung-t'ing under Pa-ling to the east of Japan,—
The water between the red banks joins with the Silver River.
In the midst are clouds with flying dragons;
Boatmen and fishermen come in to the bank;
Mountain trees all bend under the wind which raises huge waves.
His especial skill in distant prospects, none of the ancients equals:
In a foot one must consider ten thousand *li*.
How may I take sharp Ping-chou scissors
And cut off half the Wu-sung River?[16]

Thought not a painter, Tu Fu had a good opinion of himself as a calligrapher and once compared himself with the great Wang Hsi-chih (321–79).[17] His interest in calligraphy, the basic art of painting, was not less than in painting itself. His *Song of Li Ch'ao's Pa-fen and Small Seal Styles*[18] (Li Ch'ao was a maternal cousin whom he encountered late in life at K'uei-chou) is virtually a short history of Chinese script forms. In *Yang Chien Shows Me a Piece of Chang Hsü's Draft-Style* he combines a dramatic description of the force of the calligraphy with the expression of grief for a dead friend.

The man has already died;
The secrets of this "draft-style" master are hard to discover.
Now you have kindly shown me this,
The sight of it is very sad.
A mournful air arises from the thin silk;
A vast distance is opened by its old appearance.
Tinkling, sounding jades stir;
Haughtily, massed pines stand erect;
Linking hills wind in the midst;
An ocean's flood aids the brush's power.
He would in fact write on the silk before it was dyed;
The pool he wrote by was truly completely black.
Elegance and distinction were his chief aim;
In his late years his conception came to its height.
I do not know, after Chang and Wang,
Who can stand with him as a model for a hundred generations?
Oh! the genius of Eastern Wu!
His untrammelled spirit has touched His Excellency Yang's
    clear intelligence.
When His Excellency had dusted the box,
He spread out the roll and forgot to sleep or eat.
I remember how he wielded his brush,
And not only observed his powers as a drinker![19]

The poems on paintings and calligraphy are an especially distinctive group in Tu Fu's collection and are naturally of particular interest to the art historian. Yet Tu Fu was not of course writing for future art historians. A topic was a mere starting point for Tu Fu, who would proceed from it in any direction in which his thought turned. Even with so definite an object as a painting before him, he seldom confined himself to its description or appreciation, as the examples considered demonstrate.

III   *Allegorical Poems*

The representation of a poet's personal situation and feelings by analogies drawn from the careers or allusion to the writings of earlier persons is a very common feature of Chinese poetry, and Tu Fu shows abundant examples. Once the reference is found and its application understood, such analogies or allusions do not generally present great difficulty. Other forms of indirect expression of personal emotion through the symbolic usage of trees and flowers, birds, fish, and animals, are also common, and with Tu Fu no less than with other poets. The symbolic usage may be conventional or of personal invention, but here too the significance is fairly easy to apprehend. It is when the poet moves beyond symbolism of personal reference to writing in allegorical fashion of events in which he may have no direct part that serious and often insoluble difficulty may arise.

The initial problem of determining whether a poem is in fact an allegory can sometimes be very difficult. It is probable that many more allegories have been detected in Chinese poetry where none was intended than have gone unsuspected. For from the time that commentators in the Han period interpreted as political allegories the love songs of the *Book of Songs* (contents from ca. 800–600 B.C.), Chinese critics became trained to expect allegory and so continually to discover it. With any individual poet the judgment has to be guided by the general characteristics of his work. Since Tu Fu's poetry is otherwise very rarely purely descriptive and without the interpolation of the poet's thoughts, one may with reason suspect a poem which on first reading *is* only descriptive of having an allegorical intention. From here on one can only begin to guess or rather to consider whether one accepts the guesses of various commentators.

An interesting case to consider is that of the sixteen *yung-wu*[20] poems which have been placed in Tu Fu's "Lung-yu" period in 759. Some of these poems are certainly not allegories, although their language may have symbolic values. For example, *The Empty Purse.*

> The green cypress is bitter, yet still may be eaten;
> The dawn clouds are high, but still may be fed on.
> The men of the age are all without principle,
> But my way is one of hardships.
> Since we cannot cook, the well stays frozen in the morning;
> Since there are no clothes, the bed is cold at night.
> If the purse were empty, it might be ashamed,
> So I leave it one coin to take care of.[21]

The green cypress fruits and the dawn clouds are customary food for "immortals," but they are of no use to Tu Fu in his bitter poverty. The purse should not be let to feel shame, but what of its owner?

If the thing is a symbol of the man, the animal is even more likely to be. The poem entitled *The Sick Horse* in this group can be seen as an example of the range of Tu Fu's sympathy, but at the same time the degree to which he applies to the horse language which he so often uses of himself suggests that he is aiming at identification.

> For a long time I have ridden you
> In the weather's cold and the borders' remoteness.
> Amid the dust you have grown old and exhausted;
> In the lateness of the year you are sick and pitiable.
> Your points are not out of the ordinary,
> But your good temper has remained until now.
> The creature is humble but of no little significance;
> I am moved to a very deep sigh.[22]

The topics of several of these poems are believed by commentators to symbolize Tu Fu's condition. *The Melon Frame* is thought to represent his lonely, refugee-like situation.

> The bound sticks have already collapsed,
> The melon leaves have become ragged.
> Luckily, the white flowers have set their fruits;
> There is no reason for the green tendrils not to be removed.
> The chirping of the autumn insects has not ceased;

The sparrows at evening, what do they intend?
The cold weather scene now is desolate;
Man's life too has its Spring.[23]

If the commentators' understanding is correct, the symbolism is
one of tone and atmosphere; there is no close equation of detail.
But perhaps some greater precision than this is possible. Tu Fu
may have given some indication of the tendency of his thought
in the last line. The word translated "Spring" to fit the context
actually means "beginning" and is likely to evoke its opposite,
"end." The melons on the frame have fulfilled their purpose and
come to fruit, but will the poet achieve a fitting end? The ques-
tioning tone seems to be aided by the fifth and sixth lines. This
sense of anxiety for his future would accord well with his situation in late 759.

The Cricket can with some confidence be understood to symbolize his own loneliness as a traveler.

> The cricket is very tiny,
> Yet how moving are its sad notes!
> It is not happy to chirp among the grasses,
> But under the bed seeks companionship.
> Can one, long a traveler, fail to weep?
> One, once a wife, cannot sleep till dawn.
> Melancholy strings and shrill pipes
> Move us less than Nature's notes.[24]

When one takes up the companion poem to *The Cricket* (the
sixteen poems fall into eight pairs; *The Empty Purse* pairs with
The Sick Horse), *The Fire-fly*, the creature is clearly not a symbol
for the poet himself.

> Luckily you have come out from rotting weeds;
> Dare you fly near the sun?
> You are not able to illumine books,
> But can always bespot a traveler's clothes.
> Carried on the wind, you seem small outside the curtain;
> Specked with rain, you are faint by the side of the wood.
> When in the tenth month the chill frost is heavy,
> In your distress where will you turn?[25]

The commentators here discover a political allegory and as its
subject, the powerful eunuch Li Fu-kuo. If the initial identification is accepted, the details work out quite well. The "rotting

weeds" will be the eunuchs, the sun (a conventional symbol) will be the emperor. The third line will be an expression of the scholar's hostility toward the unlearned eunuch. This third line may also be regarded as containing an indication of the allegorical nature of the poem, since in the literary tradition the firefly provides the poor scholar with light to study by. The fourth line suggests that the poet holds the eunuch responsible for personal harm. The implication of the fifth and sixth lines may be furtiveness, and the last lines will express the wish for the eunuch's speedy removal.

The neatness of the explanation in this case may convince some and perhaps arouse doubt in others. None of the other poems in this group offers the same opportunity for detailed unraveling. Some, such as *Pounding Clothes*, are versions of traditional themes.

> "I know indeed that you will not return from frontier guard,
> But when autumn comes, I wipe clean the washing stone.
> We are coming to the bitter winter months,
> And I feel the more our long separation.
> How can I refuse the fatigue of washing clothes,
> All to be sent to the remoteness of the frontier wall?
> I am using all my woman's strength;
> You must listen for its sound at the sky's end."[26]

This in its title and its treatment is an "imitation" of an old *yüeh-fu* song, but to identify it as such does not make clear Tu Fu's intention in writing it. Can the wife longing for her husband at the frontier be intended as analogy for himself longing for return to the court? *The Returning Swallows* which is paired with *Pounding Clothes* can be read in a manner to lend support to this interpretation. It is necessary to understand the birds as the poet at the symbolic level and thus see him regretting his temporary withdrawal because "companions are few" (a reference to the banishment of Fang Kuan's party?), but still hoping to return.

> It is not simply to avoid the frost and snow;
> It is rather that their companions are few.
> The four seasons do not lose their order;
> In the eighth month they know they must return.
> In springtime how should they visit me?

And all the young again learn the secrets?
"If the old nest is not destroyed,
We may fly about the master."[27]

These sixteen *yung-wu* poems, apparently written at about the
same time, hard though they are to interpret with certainty, stand
out in Tu Fu's collection as a conspicuous group of poems of
symbolic or allegorical intention. These poems are all five-word
lü-shih and some number of later examples show that Tu Fu
favored this form for such poems. But as one would expect from
its general character and Tu Fu's use of it, a number of allegorical poems are to be found in the *ch'i-ku* (seven-word old form)
also. *Song of the Thin Horse,* generally placed in 758, provides a
parallel with *The Sick Horse,* given above, and to some extent
reinforces the suggestion made about that poem. The song is a
description of a horse actually seen, but at the same time the
horse seems to serve as an allegory for the banished Tu Fu.

In the eastern outskirts a thin horse makes me sad,
For his bones stand up like a low wall.
If one hobbled him and tried to move him, he would go awry.
This horse surely has no thought of prancing any more.
A close inspection of his six brands shows he has an "official" mark;
Everyone says that the army left him by the roadside.
His coat is dry with bare patches and mud-spattered;
His mane is dull and lifeless and covered with snow and frost.
Last year, unresting, he pursued the last of the rebels;
A noble horse, unless he is trained, cannot go to war.
The soldiers often ride horses from the palace stables;
I fear that this may be a sick courser.
In that time's swift racing you made a false leap;
Against being abandoned you could not guard.
When you see men, you are sad and seem to complain;
Having lost your master, you are dispirited and lusterless.
In the cold weather let roam afar, wild geese are your companions;
In the evening not stalled, crows peck at your sores.
Who for a while will care for you and grant you a final favor?
And test you again next year when the spring grass is tall?[28]

One of the latest of his *ch'i-ku, The Red Phoenix* is again an
allegory of himself.

Sir, don't you see
Of the hills between the Hsiao and the Hsiang, Heng-shan is the
   highest.

On its summit the red phoenix' note is mournful;
It turns to the side and long gazes, seeking its flock.
With wings drooping, mouth silent, mind troubled,
It looks down with pity on all birds in the nets;
The smallest sparrows still cannot escape.
It is willing to share its bamboo seeds even with the ants;
Let the owls angrily hoot as they will.[29]

This is a poem in part of strangely arrogant tone, yet made tolerable by the fact that it is the arrogance of unlimited compassion. For the greater part, Tu Fu uses symbolism and allegory in reference to himself and his own situation. Cryptic reference to events by sustained allegory proves much less common than might be expected from Tu Fu's abiding concern with current affairs. Perhaps the best example of an allegory of a current event—at least one where the commentators are in general agreement as to its application—is *Song of the Cuckoo*. On September 3, 760, former Emperor Hsüan-tsung was forced by Li Fu-kuo with a body of troops to remove from the Southern to the Western Palace in an apparent attempt to isolate him from the outer court. To this event *Song of the Cuckoo* may reasonably be referred.

Sir, have you not heard
How in former days the emperor of Shu
Changed into a cuckoo, like an old crow?
He put his young into a nest and did not feed them himself;
Until today all birds feed the cuckoo's young.
Although it is like the old rites between ruler and ministers,
He is constrained and lonely with his kin all about him.
He has become skilled at hiding away in the depths of
    the trees.
And in the fourth and fifth months utters his harsh cries.
His note is distressful, his mouth runs with blood;
Why is his complaint always *cuck-cuck?*

Were you injured that you began to express anger?
Or were you ashamed to have feathers and grieved at your
    clumsy form?
Who can predict the changes of the blue sky?
In the vicissitudes of all things what may not be?
In the vicissitudes of all things what may not be?
How should you remember all the ministers hurrying in your
    palace?[30]

For this allegory there was by good fortune the local Shu (Szechwan) legend to explain the habits of the cuckoo ready to hand. The hidden subject was a dangerous one because Su-tsung was criticized for his failure to protect his father. It was clearly a subject which could not be openly treated.

Such a poem, one feels, Tu Fu could still have included in his definition of "spontaneous."[31] He had a lasting affection for the aged Hsüan-tsung and it is likely that the news of this affair would have moved him deeply. In general, it may be said that Tu Fu had no deliberate plan at any stage in his life to write political allegories, as Po Chü-i (772–846) was to do in his early period. Allegory and symbolism were a part of the technique which he commanded to be called into service at his poetic need.

IV *Poems of Friendship*

Some of the most moving and passionate of Tu Fu's poems are addressed to his friends. Arthur Waley noted many years ago that in Chinese poetry the theme of friendship occupies relatively the place of love poetry in the literature of the West. This is a feature which will immediately strike a Westerner; to a Chinese of the past the theme of friendship was too usual to invite comment. Arthur Waley's favorite poet, Po Chü-i, enjoyed a lasting and equal friendship with Yüan Chen, but with Tu Fu the case is rather different and merits a slightly closer scrutiny than it has generally received. In spite of the large number of Tu Fu's poems which can be classified as poems of friendship, the return he received seems now remarkably slight. Poems addressed to Tu Fu which have survived amount to a mere handful. One might easily imagine that there were others that were lost, but this still does not give a very satisfactory answer. Poems addressed to him by minor poets are likely to have been lost, but among Tu Fu's friends there were major poets whose works have been substantially transmitted so that the argument of loss is not finally compelling. It seems, when one considers the evidence, that most of Tu Fu's friendships were somewhat onesided. A number of specific cases may be considered.

Something has already been said of the most notable of Tu Fu's friendships, that with Li Po.[32] After the two poems at the time of their parting in the autumn of 745 no word more came from Li Po. In the years immediately after the leave-taking, Tu Fu probably often recalled the older poet with great longing for a reunion. There are two short poems "remembering Li Po," one of which contains a very generous tribute to his poetry.

> Po in poetry is without equal;
> Soaring, his thought is uncommon:
> In pure freshness a Yü K'ai-fu;
> In surpassing excellence a Pao Ts'an-chün.
> North of the Wei are spring trees;
> East of the Kiang evening clouds.
> When with a jar of wine may we
> Again closely argue about writing.[33]

Such generosity in praise of contemporary poets is a noteworthy characteristic of Tu Fu, for it is as generally rare in China as in the rest of the world.

Tu Fu asked for a poem of farewell[34] which he wrote for another poet, K'ung Ch'ao-fu, who was leaving Ch'ang-an for the southeast, to be shown to Li Po, if K'ung encountered him. This was probably in 747. After this Li Po does not appear in his surviving poems for a further ten years. It was Li Po's misfortune during the rebellion which stirred Tu Fu's deepest compassion. The two *Dreaming of Li Po* poems have always been among his most admired.

I

> Parting by death swallows up lament;
> Parting in life is a constant sorrow.
> From the malarial lands of the South
> There is no news of the exile.
> That my friend comes into my dreams
> Shows that I forever think of him.
> But perhaps it is not your living soul;
> Since the way is so far, I cannot tell.
> Your soul came from the green of maple forests;
> Your soul returns from the darkness of the passes.
> Just now you lie in the net's meshes;
> How could you find wings?
> The sinking moon fills my house beams;
> I think it lights up your face.
> The water is deep and the waves broad:
> Do not let the dragons seize you!

II

> The floating clouds all day go by;

The wanderer for long has not come.
Three nights running I dreamt of you;
Which shows the affection of your thoughts.
When you took leave, you always hesitated;
Bitterly you said: "It is not easy to come.
On river and lake are many storms;
My boat's oar may perhaps be lost."
Going out of the gate, you scratched your
    white head,
As though thwarted in all the desires of your life.
Caps and canopies fill the capital;
This man alone is distressed.
Who says that the net is all-embracing?
When an aging man yet falls into trouble.
A thousand autumns, ten thousand years' fame—
A lonely, afterdeath affair.[35]

("Who says that the net is all-embracing?" refers to *Lao-tzu* 73:
"Heaven's net is all-embracing, wide meshed but missing nothing".) Perhaps even the style of these poems with its many reminiscences of the *Nineteen Old Poems* and the *yüeh-fu* songs of
the Han period, which Li Po had imitated, is deliberately adopted
as a further token of his feeling.

These poems have generally been assigned to the autumn of
759, but since Li Po was pardoned in the spring of that year,
they seem better placed in 758. Li Po died at T'ang-t'u (modern
Anhwei) toward the end of 762; sometime before he died Tu Fu
wrote this poem for him, with a note that lately he had had no
news of him.

I have not seen my friend Li for a long time;
His feigned madness is truly pitiable.
All the men of the age wish to kill him;
My thoughts are only of love for his talent.
Brilliant are his thousand poems;
Ruinous is his single cup of wine.
To K'uang-shan where he studied,
White-headed, well may he return.[36]

It is perhaps improbable that Li Po ever saw these poems. If
he had, how could he have replied to them? They are fine poems,
full of generosity, warmth, and pity. But pity, Li Po might have
found hard to bear. Since Li Po and Tu Fu are commonly re-

garded as the two poles of T'ang poetry, their relationship has a special interest, but in fact Tu Fu's poetical relationships with his other major contemporaries are equally onesided.

Two poems to Tu Fu have survived from Kao Shih who was with him and Li Po during the excursions in "Liang and Sung" in 744,[37] and a friend of the Ch'ang-an days and later again in Shu. Both are from this last period. One is the short poem written in 760, which seems to hint at Tu Fu's having withdrawn from public life.[38] The other was written on the seventh day of the first month (February 16) 761 and commiserates with Tu Fu on his homesickness. It ends with Kao Shih saying that he is ashamed for Tu Fu to be a wanderer while he is a prefect. Kao was at this time prefect of Shu-chou (modern Ch'ung-ch'ing). Tu Fu discovered this poem among his papers in early 770, and then wrote an answer to it, although Kao Shih had been dead for five years. Again, it was typical of Tu Fu's relationships with other poets that this reply is twice as long as Kao Shih's original. While there are thus answers by Tu Fu (one strangely late) to Kao Shih's two poems, to the various poems which Tu Fu sent to his friend there are no replies, nor, as in Li Po, is there reference to Tu Fu in any other of his poems. Very much the same situation obtains with Ts'en Shen (one poem to Tu Fu) and Wang Wei (no poems). The cases of Cheng Ch'ien and Su Yü, who would appear from Tu Fu's poems to be among his closest friends, are different for virtually none of their poems have survived.[39]

Tu Fu outlived these other famous poets and all his close friends so that one could not expect poems in mourning for him such as he wrote for Cheng Ch'ien, Su Yü,[40] and others. Yet it is strange that there is so little reciprocation of affectionate reminiscence. Although any speculation has to be very much from silence, some guess may be made. Tu Fu in his poems to or about his friends often shows that intensity and exuberance which characterize a great part of his work. One is led to wonder what he was like in actual relationships, and it must be remembered that he owed very much to the kindness of others, so that he must have aroused affection or respect in them. One suspects that he was always regarded as a strange man, oversensitive and overintense; that in spite of his obviously affectionate nature he was not very successful in personal relations. *Dreaming of Li Po* may be the expression of a deep but generally unsatisfied desire.

CHAPTER 7

By Way of Conclusion: Values and Influence

By Way of Conclusion: Values and influence

THOSE WHO SEEK and gain immortality have to pay the required price. The "thousand autumns, ten thousand years' fame" which Tu Fu clearly desired carried the penalty that he had to be the Tu Fu that individuals and groups at particular moments in history wished him to be. Tu Fu has been—not undeservedly—remarkably favored by the attention of posterity. Apart from the Confucian canonical books, no work in pre-Modern China attracted so many commentaries as Tu Fu's poetry collection. No other author gave rise to nearly so many entries in all the miscellaneous works of literary comment. There was no period in which he suffered neglect, and, in spite of the violent reaction against the past in twentieth-century China, Tu Fu has remained in a place of the greatest honor, with progressives perhaps even more than reactionaries. In 1962, the 1,250th anniversary of his birth was remembered with many publications.

If one starts with the most recent Tu Fu, one finds that there has been a marked tendency to insist that he held as active principles what were only values which developed in him and found expression in his poetry through his experience of life. To take up the position which very many twentieth-century Chinese writers on Tu Fu adopt from their reformist background, that he used poetry to put forward various ideological views, patriotism, *jen-min hsing* ("feeling for the common people"), pacificism, realism, is to produce contradictions.

He was quite obviously a patriot in a "good" sense: he loved his country and its people. At the same time he had an implicit belief in the superiority of Chinese civilization and an easy tendency toward a positive dislike of the barbarian, which the rebellion years called into fierce play. He never describes the rebels

other than as "Tatars" and the violent behavior of the Uighur
allies on the loyalist side filled him with zenophobic disgust. In
Keeping the Hua-men (i.e., the Uighurs), he regrets the necessity
of employing these barbarians: "That the Central Plain may be
cleared/We have perforce to use these creatures."[1] In recent
terminology, Tu Fu might be found guilty of "Great Han chau-
vinism," and it is perhaps surprising that Chinese Communist
writers have not been conscious of the dangers implicit in their
insistence on Tu Fu's "patriotism." All such difficulties are
avoided, if one is content to see Tu Fu's response as the natural
emotional response of a man of his upbringing and time. He does
seem to overstress the rebellion as a struggle of peoples, but this
too may only appear to be so from the terms which he uses.
Essentially, he was for the T'ang house, legitimatized by occupation of the imperial throne for nearly a century and a half and the
inheritors and current representatives of Chinese civilization and
order, and opposed to the "barbarians" who sought to destroy the
T'ang house and the order it represented. This was the nature of
his "patriotism." Feeling very deeply that the civilization and
order he knew were under serious challenge, he attacked the
threat with the terms traditional in a literature which had recorded many encounters with external invaders.

When one considers how erudite and "difficult" so much of
Tu Fu's poetry is, one can imagine that in this century of the common man his works would have had small appeal without the lucky
element of those poems in which he treats the life of humble folk in
simple language. This element is in the total small, as Po Chü-i
complained more than a thousand years ago, and certainly does
not represent a deliberate effort on Tu Fu's part to write on behalf of the people. To write of Tu Fu "fighting for the people" is
a crude misrepresentation of the poet, but it is this view of him
that has secured him so much attention in recent years. If one
takes the view that Tu Fu was writing as a kind of propagandist,
then one might indeed find him worthy of blame for devoting so
little of his work to this end. Much of the recent praise of Tu Fu
on account of his feeling for the common people is thus unsound,
since if the dogmatic criterion by which Tu Fu gains commenda-
tion were more ruthlessly applied he might instead receive cen-
sure. Until the beginning of the Cultural Revolution at least, it
has seemed to uncommitted observers that Chinese Communist

literary critics were engaged in a large-scale "whitewashing" operation with regard to the major figures from the heritage of the past. The commonest redeeming features to be discovered have been "patriotism" and "feeling for the people." If, however, one does not start out with the intention of discovering in Tu Fu the illustration of a fixed principle, one will find that his feeling for the people is but a particular aspect of his general humanity and sympathy with distress, which undoubtedly deepened with his own experience. He was conscious of the greater vulnerability of ordinary people in times of disorder because of the smallness of their resources. All the evidence suggests that he saw the suffering of the people as resulting from disorder. If "the prosperous times of K'ai-yüan" could be restored, the people's sufferings would be relieved.

War was the continual object of Tu Fu's concern in the last fifteen years of his life. He came to see the continuing fighting as the greatest of evils, and many poems can be culled from his collection for an anthology of anti-war poetry. Yet once again it is pressing the facts into too confining a mold to claim that Tu Fu had progressed to a point of adopting positive pacifist principles. Distinct stages may be traced in his attitude. The first is represented by Song of the War Carts: his coming to see that the policy of military expansion was proving costly and dangerous. In the second stage, the years of the An-Shih rebellion, although he very soon became deeply moved by the pity and horror of war, he was above all anxious that the war should be fought to a successful conclusion and, as has been seen, often offered advice on strategy in his poetry. The last years of his life, which were the aftermath years of the great rebellion, marked by Tibetan invasions and local revolts, show a profound feeling of weariness and anger that the generals were unable to bring about a lasting condition of peace. Thus, in this regard also, it seems more correct to see Tu Fu responding with a deep sensitivity to actual situations rather than giving expression to a dogmatic position.

Finally, in the recent picture of Tu Fu there is the highly approved characteristic of realism. To a large extent this is a matter of distinguishing under a different caption that part of Tu Fu's work elsewhere commended as patriotic and popular. It has already been stressed that Tu Fu had a great feeling for appropriateness of language and generally used the forms of

poetry available to him with great skill. Where a realistic treatment was required by his subject, he used language that was
simple, direct, and vivid. He was clearly not inhibited, as lesser
poets might be, by considerations of what was a fit subject for
poetry or of "poetic" language, and his poems provide examples
of the current colloquial, a feature which is very rare in later *shih*-
poetry. As a generalization, it may be said that men and events
form a much greater part of the subject matter of his poetry, as
compared with the work of many of his contemporaries, in particular of Li Po, who attracts the label of "romantic." Yet, when
one surveys the sum of his work, the use of the term "realism"
seems inappropriate to describe the greater number of his subjects or their treatment.

All the lineaments of this recent portrait of Tu Fu seem to some
degree distorted, but it is not difficult to see how the distortion
arises and to view the process with some sympathy. If current
ideology is left apart, the times through which many Chinese
scholars and literary men have lived in the twentieth century
have considerable similarities with those of Tu Fu in their com-
pound of internal disorder and external aggression so that the
instinctive bond with him is very great. The desire to find in him
the attitudes of a quite different age, to lift him out of his time
and see him as different from his period and class, is understandable, for, since the language revolution of the present century, the
move from a classical literary language to writing in an idiom
close to current speech, Tu Fu has for the first time in twelve
centuries ceased to be a model for poetry, save for those few who
continue to write classical poems. His importance must now be
that of an historical personage, and, if his poems continue to be
read by Chinese, they may soon be more commonly read in translation into modern Chinese than in the original. This need not
mean that his influence will disappear.

The position of most modern Chinese critics on Tu Fu's influence from mid-T'ang to the Ch'ing period (1644–1911) is con-
sistent with their attitude to the poet himself. They approve and
emphasize his influence upon those poets in whom, as in Tu Fu,
they discover the qualities of patriotism, love of the common
people, and realism. The catalogue of such poets under Tu Fu's
spell tends to be long and to include many minor names. While
they applaud this influence of Tu Fu's "thought" or "spirit," they

may regard his formal and linguistic influence, except in the limited area of his simple poems, as of much less importance and indeed may sometimes hint that it was unfortunate.

It is undeniable that Tu Fu's influence was enormous, both as a personality with whom later poets might sympathetically identify themselves and so quote and imitate in their own poems, and as the supreme model for poetry. For the range of his content and style made it possible for him to be father to opposite tendencies. Thus his "current affairs" poems made him the best example for the "New *Yüeh-fu*" in which Po Chü-i, Yüan Chen, and their friends sought to write poems of deliberate political allegory, in spite of the complaint of Po Chü-i that out of more than a thousand poems by Tu Fu "worthy of transmission," only thirty or forty were of the *san-li* ("Three Officer") type. While the "New *Yüeh-fu*" men, Po Chü-i in particular, aimed at simple, if veiled, language, their contemporaries, Han Yü (768–824) and some of his group, are notorious for their pursuit of the abstruse and unusual, and for them Tu Fu was an admired teacher. Han Yü is more representative of the main tendency in the ninth century toward an emphasis on elaboration of diction than Po Chü-i, and to a very large degree Tu Fu's late poetry can be seen as the great source of Late-T'ang style.

By the Sung period of the tenth to the thirteenth centuries, Tu Fu had come to rest on his pinnacle of unquestioned eminence. He was secure even against attempts to possess him. The Kiangsi School of the eleventh and twelfth centuries made him their first ancestor, but later reactions against this school did not harm his reputation. His words became part of the literature and language to a degree comparable with that of Shakespeare and the King James version of the Bible in English. But also he remained a living image leading his children on the P'eng-ya road, shouting at the boys who stole the straw blown from the Thatched Hut, and in a hundred other situations, for he was in Wordsworth's definition "a man pleased with his own passions and volitions, and who rejoices more than other men in the spirit of life that is in him."

Notes and References

Chapter One

1. 169/12/7. References are to the *Chiu-chia chu Tu shih* text printed in *A Concordance to the Poems of Tu Fu*, Harvard-Yenching Institute Sinological Series, Supplement No. 14. The first figure represents the page; the second, the *chüan* no. of the *Chiu-chia* text; the third, the serial number of the poem within the *chüan*.

2. *Ch'üan T'ang shih*, Chung-hua shu-chü ed., 1960, Vol. 2, pp. 731-740.

3. The Chinese have traditionally classified *fu* in the *wen* division of a writer's works and not in the *shih* category. Since *wen* is equated with "prose" and *shih* with "verse," it has often been said that the Chinese regard *fu* as prose, and the equivalent "rhyme-prose" has enjoyed some currency. This is not very satisfactory, as the *wen* category contains other verse forms besides *fu*. Rather it is the case that *wen* and *shih* do not correspond to the Western division of prose and verse.

4. For a translation of the complete poem see p. 78.

5. 554/36/7 and 563/36/23.

6. Feng Chih, *Tu Fu chuan*, p. 19.

7. 116/8/4B.

8. 314/19/54.

9. Feng Chih, *op. cit.*, pp. 20-21; Yoshikawa, *Shiki*, pp. 65-66. The relatives concerned were an uncle Tu Feng, police commissioner at Wu-k'ang (Hu-chou, Chekiang) and the husband (Ho Hui) of an aunt, occupying the same position in Ch'ang-shu (Kiangsu). The source of the information is Tu Fu's tomb inscription for his step-grandmother, née Lu.

10. 169/12/7. The Wangs and the Hsiehs were important families of the Southern Dynasties.

11. 314/19/53.

12. See pp. 133-40.

13. The Ku-su Terrace near modern Soochow was supposed to have been built by Ho-lu, king of Wu.

14. 478/30/47B. Hsi-ling was west of modern Hsiao-shan, Chekiang. Huai-nan was the area between the Huai River and the Yangtse.

15. Or by a single poem, if one accepts Professor Hung's placing of *Yeh-yen Tso-shih chuang* (278/18/9) in this period.

16. 170/12/7.

17. 171/12/7. The places here can no longer be identified. "Lord Su" is Su Yü (later personal name Yüan-ming, died 764. "Lord" here

and elsewhere is used to render the Chinese respect word *hou*. Ko Ch'iang was a friend of Shan Chien (253–312), minister and general at the end of the Western Chin period.

18. 167/12/4. *Po-t'ou yin* ("Song of the White-headed") is the title of a Han dynasty *yüeh-fu* song, doubtfully ascribed to Cho Wen-chün, beloved of Ssu-ma Hsiang-ju (died 117 B.C.). Tu Fu uses the expression a number of times but not necessarily with allusive reference (it would convey reproach for unfaithfulness); he seems rather to intend a melancholy reference to his own old age.

19. 215/14/2.

20. See also pp. 135-38.

21. Hung, *Tu Fu*, p. 31.

22. 272/17/16.

23. See Kao Shih, *Tung-cheng fu, Kao Ch'ang-shih chi, Ssu-pu ts'ung-k'an* ed., 1.1a.

24. See Li Po, *Liang yüan yin, Fen-lei pu-chu Li T'ai-po shih, Ssu-pu ts'ung-k'an* ed., 7.13a.

25. 4/1/3.

26. *I-hsi hsing* (223/15/1) and *Hsi-yu* (75/5/3).

27. 271/17/14. The names of guest and host afford an opportunity for a pun, since there was an ancient wine-maker Tu K'ang and an earlier hermit Chang, famous for his pears.

28. *Chi Li Shih-erh Po erh-shih yün* (338/20/44).

29. See p. 30.

30. 207/14/1E.

31. 277/18/6. Yin K'eng was a Southern Dynasties poet (fl. mid-sixth century).

32. 272/17/17. Ko Hung (234–305) is the famous alchemist of the Chin period.

33. 2/1/1.

34. The ministry of personnel (*Li pu*) came under Wei Chi's authority as left secretary.

35. The exact year of Tu Fu's marriage can only be (and has been variously) guessed at.

36. Tzu-chien is the courtesy name of Ts'ao Chih (192–232).

37. "Going singing" (*hsing-ko*) is an expression used to represent the indifference of the typical hermit (e.g., Chieh-yü whom Confucius encounters in the *Analects*) to the world. In the next line of the poem I emend *san-shih* to *i* (already) *shih*.

38. Master Kung is Kung Yü (123–44 B.C.) famous for his friendship with Wang Chi; for both see *Han-shu* 72. Yüan Hsien is the disciple of Confucius, famous for his cheerful endurance of extreme poverty.

39. 206/14/1D.

40. 269/17/9.
41. 289/18/28A.
42. See note 3 above.
43. The answer depends on whether the *fu, The Eagle* dates from before 751. The memorial with which it was submitted contains an ambiguous phrase, understood by some to refer to Tu Fu's age, i.e., "nearly 40" and by others to refer to a period of years i.e. "for nearly forty years."
44. 134/9/23. The difference in the names of the palaces arises from Tu Fu's using in the former case a Han dynasty name (as he commonly does) for a T'ang actuality.
45. *Ibid.*
46. *Feng Hsi-yüeh fu (The Investiture of the Hua Mountain).*
47. 293/19/1.
48. 171/12/7. Aspens are regular graveyard trees.
49. 24/2/3.
50. 162/11/27..
51. See also pp. 108-11.
52. 9/1/12.
53. See Waley, *Li Po,* pp. 34-36.
54. 24/2/4.
55. See *Chin Feng Hsi-yüeh fu piao.*
56. 13/1/16.
57. 20/1/24.
58. 34/2/12.
59. 37/2/16.
60. 3/1/2.
61. 291/18–34. "To bend my back" is a common allusion to the story in the biography of T'ao Yüan-ming (365–427) of how he gave up his magistracy at P'eng-tse in 405 rather than bow down before a petty official.
62. 296/19/11.
63. 287/18/25.

Chapter Two

1. 38/2/16. Ch'ih-yu, in ancient legend the antagonist of the Yellow Emperor, was later revered as a god of war. Commentators offer a variety of explanations of "Ch'ih-yu banners"; in view of the following line nothing more elaborate than "military banners" seems to be required. Wei and Ho, surnames of maternal relatives of Han emperors, are used to represent the Yangs.
2. See E. G. Pulleyblank, *The Background of the Rebellion of An Lu-shan,* chapter 6.
3. 40/2/17.
4. 58/3/19.

5. 295/19/6.

6. See pp. 107-8.

7. 43/2/21. The Staying-Autumn Gate was the west gate of the palace park, by which Hsüan-tsung fled. "The stout lads of Shuo-fang" refers to Ko-shu Han's defeated army; "men of Hua-men" were the Uighur cavalry who throughout played a prominent part against the rebels. The Five Tombs were those of the first five T'ang emperors.

8. 44/2/22.

9. 45/2/23.

10. 295/19/5.

11. 57/3/18.

12. 295/19/9.

13. 296/19/10.

14. 43/2/20. "The First Lady of the Chao-yang Palace" was Chao Fei-yen, concubine and later empress of the Han emperor Ch'eng (reigned 32–7 B.C.), but she is here simply a substitute for Yang Kuei-fei. Ma-wei post station, where Yang Kuei-fei was killed, was near the Wei River; Hsüan-tsung would have gone through the Sword Pass on his way to Ch'eng-tu.

15. 299/19/14. Feng-hsiang was south of Mt. Ch'i. The "Han garden" means the palace park at Ch'ang-an. The "aura of Nan-yang" is an appearance of the restoration of the dynasty: the allusion is to Liu Hsiu (Emperor Kuang-wu) who restored the Han dynasty in 25 A.D.; he was a native of Nan-yang and also at one point commandant of services. T'ai-po ("Great Whiteness"; it is permanently snow-capped) and Wu-kung are names of mountains near Feng-hsiang.

16. This translation was coined by Arthur Waley in his *Life and Times of Po Chü-i*.

17. 46/3/1.

18. 52/3/8.

19. 48/3/3. T'ien-wu was a sea-god of monstrous form.

20. Ts'en Shen's post was that of *Yu pu-ch'üeh* ("Right Repairer of Deficiences").

21. 71/4/18.

22. I have not included a translation of this famous poem here, since the amount of annotation required would be out of proportion.

23. 307/19/30. The unicorn in the first poem is of stone.

24. 306/19/25B.

25. 306/19/26.

26. 328/20/24.

27. 17/1/20.

28. Wang Ssu-shih, *Tu i*, vol. 2, p-103a.

29. *The Parting of the Aged* (*Ch'ui-lao pieh*) refers to winter. Professor Hung therefore places it on the outward journey to Lo-yang.

30. 53/3/9. Hsiang-chou was the new name given to Yeh in 758. Tu Fu is liable to follow poetic convenience in using current or previous place names: he returns to Yeh in *The Shih-hao Officer.* "The minister" is Kuo Tzu-i.

31. 53/3/10. The small walls referred to in the fourth line must be on the top of the pass. The "battle of the T'ao-lin" refers to Ko-shu Han's disaster of 756.

32. 54/3/11.

Chapter Three

1. 56/3/15.

2. 73/4/20.

3. 334/20/41.

4. 318/20/1A.

5. 90/6/4. Han-yüan was a district of T'ung-ku.

6. 96/6/17. The worthy of the first line is Mo Ti, fifth century, B.C. philosopher and founder of the Mohist school. The sage is Confucius.

7. See pp. 131-33.

8. 80/5/12A. I have followed a different arrangement of these series from the Chiu-chia text, in which my third poem (T'ao Ch'ien) appears as 83/5/14C.

9. 75/5/2C.

10. It does not seem to me that Tu Fu is suggesting that he wishes to emulate the "Old Man in the Deerskin" (a typical hermit) in his indifference to the world, though this is perhaps the usual understanding.

11. 96/6/16.

12. Lien P'o was a successful general of the northern state of Chao in the first half of the third century B.C.

13. See also pp. 141-44.

14. 322/20/2.

15. The famous *Dreaming of Li Po* (two poems; see pp. 147-48) and *Twenty Rhymes to Li Po* (338/20/44).

16. 80/5/11 and 381/24/11.

17. 101/6/28.

18. Some understand the expression translated "patron," *chu-jen,* as indicating Tu Fu himself, but this seems an awkward reading.

19. 341/21/2. Shan-yin was at the other end of the Yangtse in modern Chekiang.

20. 344/21/10. Some place this poem in 762 on account of the statements of the poem *To be Inscribed on My Thatched Hut Beyond the River,* for which see p. 78.

21. 363/22/25.

22. 343/21/5.

23. 346/21/15.

24. 345/21/12.

25. 344/21/8.

26. 122/8/14. *Shang-yüan* will indicate 760 and *Pao-ying,* 762.

27. 111/7/15.

28. 348/21/23.

29. 136/10/2.

30. It is commony placed in 761.

31. 137/10/3.

32. 356/22/2. Tu Fu has a note that the "old man of O-mei" was "a recluse in the Eastern Hills." O-mei, one of China's most famous mountains, is southwest of Ch'eng-tu.

33. 357/22/10.

34. 114/8/1. Hsiao-Hsiang indicates an area corresponding to the present province of Hunan. Nan-hai is modern Kwangtung.

35. 114/8/2.

36. 104/7/4.

37. 375/23/17.

38. 375/23/21. "Three reigns": those of the Hsüan-tsung, Su-tsung, and Tai-tsung emperors.

39. 364/22/31.

40. *Ch'üan T'ang-wen* c. 457.

41. 143/10/18.

42. 382/24/14. Chi-pei indicates the area of modern northern Hopei, the starting point of the rebellion.

43. P'u Ch'i-lung in his commentary to the poem, p. 628.

44. Professor Hung (*Notes,* p. 91) resolves the difficulty by declaring *Ninth Day* (411/26/40) to be spurious, which is a drastic step. I suggest that some of the difficulty is caused by understanding the "three months" of the poem *Leaving Lang-chou* (133/9/19) too literally. It would not be outside Tu Fu's practice to mean by this a little over one month (i.e., one complete month and a few days of the preceding and following months).

45. 198/13/36.

46. See 410/26/33.

47. It was the same post he had filled in Hua-chou, but the ranking was slightly higher.

48. 143/10/18.

49. 144/10/19.

50. See p. 92.

51. 405/26/13.

52. 134/9/23.

53. 407/26/24. "The Peach Blossom Spring" means simply "hermitage." "Three Shu" (here meaning Ch'eng-tu) is used to balance "six years" in the next line. The Stone Mirror, a rock near Ch'eng-tu,

according to legend, marked the grave of a mountain spirit who had been the concubine of a ruler of Shu. The Snow Mountains are west of modern Sung-p'an, Szechwan; Mt. Min is the principal peak.

54. 420/27/27. Yü was the great legendary hero who regulated the waters of China by his labors.

55. 487/31/4.

56. See pp. 113-9.

57. 432/28/19B.

58. 520/33/5.

59. 541/35/1.

60. 229/15/12. The Hsiao flows into the Hsiang northwest of Yün-ling, Hunan; the Hsiang flows into the Tung-t'ing Lake. The Mo-yu were a minority people living in this area; the name means "exempt from *corvée*."

61. 395/25/12.

62. 226/15/7.

63. Tu Fu's death, like many details of his life, became the subject of disputes. According to Yüan Chen's tomb inscription, he had been temporarily buried in Yüeh-yang (Yüeh-chou) before removal to the family graveyard in 813. It is likely that he died in or near Yüeh-chou.

Chapter Four

1. 415/27/10.

2. 486/31/1.

3. 155/11/15. I read *liu* instead of the *hsiu* of the Chiu-chia text.

4. 476/30/44.

5. Wang Ssu-shih, *Tu i*, vol. 4, p. 303b.

6. See p. 29.

7. 556/36/12.

8. 409/26/30.

9. 479/30/47G.

10. 494/31/27B.

11. See p. 29.

12. 337/20/43.

13. 353/21/38.

14. See *Nan-shih, Po-na* ed. 19.16a.

15. 301/19/19.

16. 360/22/19.

Chapter Five

1. In T'ang poetry the language is still almost completely monosyllabic, though not a 100 per cent. Purists may prefer to talk of five syllables or pentasyllabic, etc., but to those familiar with other poetry of other places and times, in which a syllable does not equate with a word, such usage, if not misleading, is at least unhelpful, since it does

not call up the great emphasis of T'ang poetry in balancing *word* with *word*, e.g., "green" with "yellow," "hills" with "birds," "encircle" with "fly."

2. These figures are taken from Hsiao Ti-fei, *Tu Fu yen-chiu*, vol. 1, p. 128.

3. See pp. 35-36.

4. 186/13/14. For (Wang) Chao-chün see p. 114.

5. 111/7/16. "Southern Hill bean shoots" and "Blue Gate melon field" are common allusions belonging to the terminology of hermitage; they imply extreme poverty.

6. See p. 37.

7. 108/7/10.

8. See pp. 61-62.

9. 471/30/35.

10. 467/30/32.

11. See p. 000.

12. 368/23/3.

13. 359/22/18.

14. 404/26/5.

15. 487/31/6.

16. 354/21/44.

17. 409/26/26C.

18. Hsiao Ti-fei, *Tu Fu yen-chiu*, vol. 2, p. 156.

19. 134/9/22. Yü-chou is modern Chungking; K'ai-chou, modern K'ai-hsien, Szechwan. Lo (Camel) Valley led from modern Shensi into Szechwan.

20. 295/19/7.

21. 418/27/17.

Chapter Six

1. This is the *Fen-men chi-chu Tu Kung-pu shih*, printed in the *Ssu-pu ts'ung-k'an*.

2. For the translation of the travel part of *P'eng-ya Road* see p. 49.

3. 48/3/3. See also p. 58. The "people of Ch'in" would be those in the area of modern Shensi.

4. 93/6/14. Ni-kung (lit., "mud work") Mountain was probably an alternative name for the Black Mud Range, northwest of T'ung-ku.

5. 97/6/18. The Tree-bark Range is east of T'ung-ku. Chestnut Pavilion was the hamlet east of T'ung-ku where Tu Fu had been staying. Phoenix Village would have been near Phoenix Mountain, a notable feature of the scenery of T'ung-ku district. The Five Peaks are the five sacred mountains of China. Tu Fu will be referring in K'un-lun to the mythological mountains, abode of immortals, of which Hsüan-pu was a peak, rather than to the actual K'un-lun Mountains.

6. 98/6/21. Flying Immortals Railed Way was near modern Lüeh-yang. Shensi. T'u-men has not been identified.

7. 98/6/23. Dragon Gate Railed Way was near modern Kuang-yüan, Szechwan. Ch'ü-t'ang is one of the Yangtse gorges; Ta-yü is the name of a range dividing modern Kiangsi and Kwangtung provinces.

8. See Shen Te-ch'ien, *Shuo-shih ts'ui-yü*, quoted in Ch'en Yu-ch'in, "Man t'an Tu Fu ti t'i-hua shih," *Tu Fu yen-chiu lun-wen chi*, II, p. 268.

9. 121/8/12. Wu of Wei was Ts'ao Ts'ao (155–220). Madam Wei (Wei Shuo) was traditionally the teacher of Wang Hsi-chih (Right General Wang; 321–79), one of the most famous calligraphers. The quotations in the next lines are words of Confucius from the *Analects*. The painting which Ts'ao Pa retouched was "Twenty-four Statesmen of the Mist-Soaring Pavilion," painted by the great Yen Li-pen (died 673) in 643. The Dukes of Pao and O were Generals Tuan Chih-yüan (598–642) and Yü-ch'ih Ching-te.

10. 11/1/14. Yao-niao and Hua-liu were "thousand-*li* a day runners" of earlier times. Wang Liang is the prototype of the master horse trainer; Po Lo was renowned for his skill in judging the ability of horses by their appearance.

11. 106/7/7. "Unicorns" (written with the horse radical) like "dragons" were simply outstanding horses.

12. 128/9/9. The painter of this mural, Hsüeh Chi (648–718) was noted for mixing the "flower and bird" and "human figure" genres, and also for his paintings of cranes. Tu Fu saw this work at T'ung-ch'üan, southeast of Tzu-chou in the winter of 762. Ch'ing-t'ien (modern Chekiang) was famous for cranes.

13. 141/10/13.

14. 177/12/15. Han-yüan was the name of a palace.

15. 64/4/8.

16. 107/7/8. Fang-hu was like the K'un-lun a mythological mountain. Pa-ling is a mountain near Yüeh-yang on the eastern side of the Tung-t'ing Lake. The "Silver River" is one of the various names for the Milky Way. Ping-chou (modern T'ai-yüan, Shansi) was famous for the making of scissors. The Wu-sung River is in modern Kiangsu.

17. See 378/23/37.

18. 216/14/3.

19. 176/12/14. Chang and Wang are Chang Chih (second century A.D.) and Wang Hsi-chih. Chang Hsü was a native of Soochow, hence Tu Fu calls him "the genius of Eastern Wu." He appears as one of the "immortals" in *Song of the Eight Immortals of the Wine-cup*, one of the most famous poems in Tu Fu's collection. I side with those who consider it spurious.

20. See also p. 73.
21. 329/20/28.
22. 329/20/29.
23. 326/20/18.
24. 325/20/14.
25. 326/20/15.
26. 325/20/13.
27. 325/20/12.
28. 60/4/1.
29. 227/15/9.
30. 104/7/3.
31. See pp. 102-4.
32. See also pp. 23-27.

33. 280/18/11. Yü K'ai-fu is Yü Hsin (513–81), whom Tu Fu greatly admired; K'ai-fu is an abbreviation of the title K'ai-fu i t'ung ta chiang-chün (lit., "Establishing a headquarters with ceremonies equal to those of the generalissimo"), which went with his office as a general under the Northern Chou dynasty. Pao Ts'an-chün is Pao Chao (ca. 420–66), who was famous for his *yüeh-fu* songs; Ts'an-chün is from his office as a military aide.

34. 21/2/1.
35. 79/5/10.

36. 381/24/12. K'uang-shan seems more likely to be the Ta-k'uang shan in Chang-ming, Szechwan rather than the famous Lu-shan (sometimes K'uang-lu shan) in Kiangsi.

37. See p. 24.
38. See p. 76.

39. *Ch'üan T'ang-shih* c. 255 contains two poems by Su Yü and one by Cheng Ch'ien.

40. See p. 127.

Chapter Seven

1. 57/3/17.

Selected Bibliography

PRIMARY SOURCES

Editions of Tu Fu's Works (only those generally available in recent reprintings are listed).

Chiu-chia chu Tu shih in *A Concordance to the Poems of Tu Fu*, Harvard-Yenching Institute Sinological Series, Supplement No. 14. 3 vols. Taipei repr.: 1967.

Fen-men chi-chu Tu Kung-pu shih, Ssu-pu ts'ung-k'an ed.

Ch'ien Ch'ien-i. *Ch'ien chu Tu shih*. 2 vols. Shanghai: Chung-hua shu-chü, 1958.

Ch'ou Chao-ao. *Tu Shao-ling chi hsiang-chu*. 2 vols. Basic Sinological Series. Commercial Press.

P'u Ch'i-lung. *Tu Tu hsin chieh*. 3 vols. Peking: Chung-hua shu-chü, 1961.

Yang Lun. *Tu shih ching ch'üan*. 10 ts'e. Ch'eng-tu: Szechwan jen-min ch'u-pan she, 1957.

Commentaries without text.

Wang Ssu-shih. *Tu i*. 6 ts'e. Chung-hua shu-chü, 1962.

Shih Hung-pao. *Tu Tu shih shuo*. Shanghai: Chung-hua shu-chü, 1962.

SECONDARY SOURCES

Modern Chinese Studies

FENG CHIH. *Tu Fu chuan*. Peking: Jen-min wen-hsüeh ch'u-pan she, 1953. A biography of the poet, with some emphasis on his poetry.

—————. Ed. *Tu Fu shih hsüan*. Peking: Tso-chia ch'u-pan she, 1956. A selection of some 260 poems with brief notes.

FU KENG-SHENG. *Tu Fu shih lun*. Shanghai: Shanghai lien-ho ch'u-pan she, 1954. Essays on Tu Fu's "feeling for the people," patriotism, realism, etc.; a substantial representative of post-1949 attitude to Tu Fu.

—————. *Tu shih san-i*. Sian: Tung-feng wen-i ch'u-pan she, 1959. Very free, diffuse translations of ninety-six poems into modern Chinese, arranged with explanatory matter to illustrate aspects of Tu Fu's life.

HSIAO TI-FEI. *Tu Fu yen-chiu.* 2 vols. Tsinan: Shan-tung jen-min ch'u-pan she, 1956. Vol. 1 contains study of life, thought, and works of the poet; Vol. 2 a selection of 266 poems (some difference from Feng Chih's selection and annotation much more detailed).

HUA WEN-HSUAN (comp.). *Tu Fu chüan.* Part I (T'ang-Sung). 3 vols. Peking: Chung-hua shu-chü, 1964. An omnibus of references to Tu Fu and his works. Part I only has appeared.

SZECHWAN SHENG WEN-SHIH YEN-CHIU KUAN (comp.). *Tu Fu nien-p'u.* Ch'eng-tu: Szechwan jen-min ch'u-pan she, 1958. A chronology of Tu Fu's life and works, fairly largely based on Feng Chih and Wen I-to.

Tu Fu yen-chiu lun-wen chi. 3 vols. Peking: Chung-hua shu-chü, 1962–63. Collection of reprinted articles on Tu Fu; Vol. 1 1922–49; Vol. 2 1949–61; Vol. 3 1962. Vol. 3 also contains a valuable Tu Fu bibliography.

WEN I-TO. *Shao-ling hsien-sheng nien-p'u hui-chien* in *Wen I-to ch'üan-chi,* Vol. 3. Shanghai: K'ai-ming shu-chü, 1948.

YEH CHIA-YING. *Tu Fu ch'iu-hsing pa-shou chi-shuo. (Chung-hua ts'ung-shu)* Taipei, 1966.

Japanese Translations and Studies

Chûgoku bungakuho. Vol. 17 (1962). Special number of Tu Fu studies.

KUROGAWA YOICHI. *To Ho. (Chûgoku shijin senshû* No. 9). 2 vols. Tokyo: Iwanami shoten, 1957. A small selection of best-known poems.

MORI KAINAN. *Toshi kôgi.* 3 vols. Tokyo: Bunkaidô, 1912. Pioneer modern Japanese study.

SUZUKI TORAO, *To-Shôryô shishû.* 4 vols. in *Zoku kokuyaku kambun taisei* series. Tokyo: 1928–31. Complete translation.

TOKI ZENMARO. *Shinshaku To Ho shisen.* 4 vols. Tokyo: Shunshûsha, 1955–61. Selection of Tu Fu's poems of various periods with similar poems selected from other poets.

YOSHIKAWA KOJIRO. *To Ho shiki.* Vol. 1. Tokyo: Chikuma shobô, 1950.

————. *To Ho nôto.* Tokyo: Sôgensha, 1952. Miscellaneous studies of biographical details and poems.

————. *To Ho. (Sekai koten bungaku zenshû* No. 28) Vol. 1. Tokyo: Chikuma shobô, 1967. Extensively annotated translation of poems to end of 755.

Works in Western Languages

HAWKES, DAVID. *A Little Primer of Tu Fu.* London: Oxford University Press, 1967

HUNG, WILLIAM. *Tu Fu: China's Greatest Poet.* With a supplementary volume of Notes. Cambridge: Harvard University Press, 1952.

PULLEYBLANK, E. G. *The Background of the Rebellion of An Lu-shan.* London: Oxford University Press, 1955.

SCHAFER, EDWARD H. *The Golden Peaches of Samarkand: A Study of T'ang Exotics.* Berkeley: University of California Press, 1963.

SCHAFER, EDWARD H. *The Vermilion Bird: T'ang Images of the South.* Berkeley: University of California Press, 1967.

VON ZACH, ERWIN. *Tu Fu's Gedichte.* (Harvard-Yenching Institute Studies, VIII). 2 vols. Cambridge: Harvard University Press, 1952.

WALEY, ARTHUR. *The Poetry and Career of Li Po.* New York: Macmillan, 1950.

Index

Academy of Assembled Worthies.
  See Chi-hsien Yüan
Allegory in Chinese poetry, 73, 140
An Ch'ing-hsü, 54, 59, 62, 64
An Lu-shan, 16, 34, 46–47, 54
An-Shih rebellion, 46, 86

Book of Songs, 140
Bright Radiance Palace, 32
Brocade River (or Stream; at Ch'eng-
  tu), 75, 111
Buddhism, 23
Byron, 45

Central Asia, Chinese power in, 15,
  35
Ch'an (river), 18
Chang, Hermit, 25
Ch'ang-an, 15 *et passim*
Chang Ch'ien, 116
Chang Chih, 139
Chang Ching-shun, 135–36
Chang Hao, 55, 60, 62
Chang Hsü, 139
Chang Liang, 60
Chang Piao, 74
Ch'ao-fu, 41
Chao-yang Palace, 53
Cheng Ch'ien, 42, 54, 59, 74, 92,
  126–27, 149
Ch'eng-tu, 75 *et passim*
Ch'eng Yüan-chen, 87
Ch'en Lin, 100, 101
Ch'en-liu, 24
Ch'en-t'ao, 51
Ch'en Tzu-ang, 106
Che River, 19
Chestnut Pavilion, 68–69, 132
Chestnut Village, 69
Chi (ancient minister), 40–41
Ch'i (ancient minister), 40–41
Ch'i (mountain), 54

Chia Chih, 60, 62, 73
Chia I, 92
Chiang-ling, 60, 95, 113, 114
Chiang-ning, 19
Ch'iang Village, 49, 56
Ch'ien-fu lun, 100
Chien-nan Province, 88, 90
Chi-hsien Yüan, 32–33
Ch'i-Liang style, 106
Ch'in, First Emperor of, 19
Ch'in, Lady of, 36, 48
Ch'in-chou, 67–68, 131
Ching-chao, 15, 20, 88
Ching-chou, 62
Ch'ing-fan, 51
Ching River, 38, 39, 130
Ch'ing-t'ien, 136
Chi-tzu (Tu Fu's son), 53, 126
Chuang-tzu, 23
Ch'ü-chiang. *See* Curving Stream
Chüeh-chü poems, 106, 107–8, 119–25
Chu-ko Liang, 70–71, 93, 110,
  114–15, 123
Chung-chou, 93
Chung-li, 52
Chung-nan Hills, 30
Ch'ü-t'ang Gorge, 21, 118, 133
Ch'u-tz'u, 99
Ch'ü Yüan, 99
Coir palms, 82
Cold Food Festival, 43
College for the Extension of Litera-
  ture, 42
Complete T'ang Poems, 14
Confucian society, 76, 98
Curving Stream, 53, 61, 118

Defense Against Ridicule, 76
Department of State Affairs, 28, 116
Dew-receivers (statues), 117
Diamond Sutra, 23
Double Ninth Festival, 39, 43, 93

Double Third Festival, 36
Dragon Gate, 133
Dragon Pool, 69

Early-T'ang period of poetry, 112
East Nang Stream, 94
East Village, 94
Examinations, 17, 20, 27

Fang-hu (mythological mountain), 138
Fang Kuan, 51, 55, 60, 62, 73, 86–87, 143
Fan-yang, 47, 59, 62
Feng-chi Post Station, 84
Feng-hsiang, 54, 55, 56, 59, 60, 130
Feng-hsien, 39, 43, 47, 49
Feng Shao-cheng, 138
Firewood gathering women of K'uei-chou, 109
Five Tombs (of T'ang emperors), 51, 117
Flower Calyx Tower, 118
Flower Washing Stream, 75
Fu, 16, 32, 99
Fu-chou, 49, 50, 56, 131
Fu-sang, 19

Grand Canal, 15
Great Mystery Classic, 76

Han, Lady of, 36, 48
Han-chou, 86
Han Kan, 135
Han River, 82
Han Yü, 154
Han-yüan (district of T'ung-ku), 68
Han-yüan (palace), 138
Heng-chou, 96–97
Heng-shan, 144
Herdboy and Weaving Girl (stars), 43
High-T'ang period of poetry, 16, 107, 112, 119
Ho-hsi, 41
Ho-lu, king of Wu, 19
Ho-nan Province, 86
Ho-pei Province, 47, 86
Ho Sun, 103
Ho-tung (border command), 47

Ho-yang, 64, 66
Hsiang-chou, 65
Hsiang River, 96, 144
Hsiang-yang, 86
Hsiao Ho, 60, 115
Hsiao-Hsiang tangerine trees, 82
Hsiao River, 96, 144
Hsieh family, 19
Hsieh Hui-lien, 105
Hsieh Ling-yün, 100, 102, 103, 105
Hsieh T'iao, 100, 103
Hsi K'ang, 70–71
Hsi-ko, *See* West Pavilion
Hsi-ling, 20
Hsin-an, 65
Hsin T'ang-shu, 67
Hsüan-pu (peak of K'un-lun mountains), 132
Hsüan-tsung, Emperor, 15–16, 23, 31, 34, 35, 45, 48, 50, 53, 59, 75, 84, 134, 137, 145–46
Hsü Chih-tao, 85
Hsüeh Chi, 136–37
Hsüeh Chü, 74
Hsü Kan, 100
Hsün-hsia, 17
Hsü Yu, 41
Hua-ch'ing Palace, 45
Hua Ching-ting, 83–84
Hua-chou, 62, 64, 65, 67, 103
Huai-nan, 20
Hua-liu (horse), 136
Hua-men, *See* Uighurs
Hua Peak, 47

Imperial University, 42
I River, 23
I Yin, 115

Jade-flower Dapple (imperial horse), 135
Japan, 19, 139
Jen-min hsing, 150
Juan Yü, 100
Ju-chou, 62
Jui-tsung, Emperor, 39
Jung-chou, 93

K'ai-yüan (reign period), 18, 134
Kao Hsien-chih, 35

Kao Shih, 24, 34, 41, 42, 48, 60, 68, 74, 76, 85, 90, 149
Kao-t'ang fu, 114
Keats, 127
Keng-sang-tzu, 23
Kiangsi school of poetry, 154
Ko Ch'iang, 21
Ko Hung, 26, 76
Kokonor, 36
Korea, 16
Ko-shu Han, 41, 42, 48, 66
Kou-chien, king of Yüeh, 19
K'uai-chi, 19
K'uang Heng, 116
K'uang-shan, 148
K'uei-chou, 93 *et passim*
Ku K'ai-chih, 19
Kung-an, 95
K'ung Ch'ao-fu, 147
K'ung Jung, 100
Kung-sun Shu (White Emperor), 93
K'ung-t'ung (mountains), 47
Kung Yü, 30
K'un-lun (mountains), 47, 132, 138
K'un-ming Lake, 118
Kuo, Lady of, 36, 48
Kuo, Prefect of Hua-chou, 62
Kuo Tzu-i, 64, 87
Ku-su Terrace, 19

Lament for the South, 101
Lang-chou, 87
Lan-t'ien, 94, 95
Lao-tzu, 23, 118
Lao-tzu, 148
Late-T'ang poetry, 134, 154
Li Ch'ao, 139
Li Chih-fang, 25, 87
Li Chin, Prince of Ju-yang, 31
Li Chin-su, 95
Lieh-tzu, 23
Lien P'o, 72
Li family (imperial), 14–15, 23
Li Fu-kuo, 60, 84, 87, 142, 145
Li Heng, *See* Su-tsung
Li Ho, 95
Li Hsien, 31
Li Huan, 83
Li Lin, Prince of Yung, 59–60, 83

Li Lin-fu, 27, 36, 42, 46
Li Ling, 99
Ling-wu, 48, 49, 51
Linked series poems, 112–13
Lin-tzu, 25
Li Po, 23–27, 34, 36, 59–60, 74, 83, 107, 119, 146–49, 153
Li-shan, 45, 137, 138
Liu, police commissioner at Feng-hsien, 138
Liu Chen, 100
Liu Hsiang, 116
Liu Pei, First Ruler of Shu, 93, 110, 114
Li Yung, 25, 28, 30
Lo Pin-wang, 106
Lo River, 18
Lotus Flower Small Garden, 118
Lo-yang, 15 *et passim*
Lu Chao-lin, 106
Lu-chün, *See* Yen-chou
Lung-men Gorge, 23
Lun-shih chüeh-chü, 106
Lü Shang, 115
Lü-shih poems, 50, 107-8
Lu-tzu Pass, 52

Ma-i Prefecture, 72
Ma-wei Post Station, 48
Ma Yüan, 101
Mei-pei Lake, 118
Mien-chou, 83, 86, 137
Min River, 93
Mist-Soaring Pavilion, 134
Mo-yu (people), 96
Mu, Emperor of Chou, 117

Nang-hsi, 94
Nang Stream, 94
Nan-hai lichees, 82
Nan-yang, 123
Nan-Yüeh, 101, 118
"New *Yüeh-fu*," 154
Nineteen Old Poems, 148

O, Duke of, 134
"Old forms" of *shih* poetry, 107, 108
Old Man in the Deerskin (hermit), 71

O-mei (mountain), 81

Pa-chou, 62
P'ai-lü poems, 107–8, 125–26
Pa-ling, 139
Pamirs, 16
Pan Ku, 16
Pao, Duke of, 134
Pao Chao, 147
Peach Blossom Spring, 33, 91, 130
P'ei, Madam (Tu Fu's aunt), 15, 22
Pei-hai, 25
P'ei Jung-chi, 15
P'eng-chou, 79
P'eng-lai, 34
P'eng-lai Palace, 32, 82, 117
P'eng-yüan, 51, 52
Phoenix Village, 132
Pin-chou, 56, 62, 130
Ping-chou, 132
P'ing-lu (border command), 47
P'i-p'a (musical instrument), 114
Pi Yao, 74
Po Chü-i, 146, 151, 154
Po Mao-lin, 94
Po-shui, 39, 47, 49
"Promoted Worthy" hats, 134
P'u Ch'i-lung, 84
Purple Pavilion Peak, 118
Purple Terrace, 114

Queen Mother of the West, 117

Radiant Concubine, *See* Wang Chao-chün
Revolts, local military, 83, 97

San-ch'uan (district in Fu-chou), 55
Shan-yin, 75
Shao-ling (in Tu-ling), 53
Shen-chou, 87
Shih Ch'ao-i, 86
Shih-hao (village), 65
Shih poetry (contrasted with *fu*), 59
Shih Ssu-ming, 46, 59, 62, 64
Shou-yang Hills, 22
Shu (modern Szechwan), 78, 90, 91, 93, 115, 146
Shu-chou, 149

Shuo-fang (border command), 50
Snow Mountains, 91, 111
Song of the White-headed (*Po-t'ou yin*), 21
Soochow, 19
Southern Capital (Ch'eng-tu), 74, 75, 77
Southern Dynasties, 18, 19
Southern Fragrance Hall, 134
Southern Palace, 145
South Park, 53
Stone Mirror (rock), 91
Sui dynasty, 15
Sung-chou, 24
Sung Yü, 113–14
Su Shih, 133
Su-tsung, Emperor, 48, 51, 52, 54, 59, 60, 84, 146
Su Wu, 99
Su Yü (Su Yüan-ming), 21, 42, 59, 92, 126–27, 149
Sword Pass, 53, 85, 86

T'ai-chou, 59, 127
T'ai-hsüan ching. See Great Mystery Classic
T'ai-po Hills, 51, 54
T'ai-tsung, Emperor, 15
T'ai-yüan, 52
Talas River, 35
T'an-chou, 97
T'ang (founder of Shang dynasty), 115
T'ang empire, 15–16
Tangerines, 81
T'ang-t'u, 148
Tang-yang, 95
T'ao Ch'ien, *See* T'ao Yüan-ming
Taoism, 23
Tao-te-ching, 23
T'ao Yüan-ming, 69, 71, 77, 80, 89, 100, 102
Ta-yü (mountains), 133
Teng-lou fu, 92
Tibet, 16
Tibetans, 68, 87, 90, 95, 97
Tiger Cliff, 69
T'i-hua shih, 133
Tones in poetry, 107

Tongking, 15
Tree-bark Range, 132
Ts'ai Yung, 100
Tsan, Abbot, 68
Ts'ao Chih (Tzu-chien), 30, 100
Ts'ao Pa, 134–35
Ts'ao P'ei, 100
Ts'ao Shen, 115
Ts'ao Ts'ao (Emperor Wu of Wei), 100, 101, 134
Ts'en Shen, 39, 42, 60–61, 68, 74, 149
Tso-chuan, 13
Ts'ui family, 14–15, 39, 47
Ts'ui Kuang-yüan, 83–84
Ts'ui Shang, 16
Tuan Tzu-chang, 83

Tu Fu, ancestry, 13–14; ATTITUDES: Confucian, 80, 100, 102; patriotism, nature of, discussed, 150–51; to Buddhism, 45; to foreign peoples, 150–51; to hunting and physical prowess, 20–22; to patronage, 28–32; to poetry, 73, 98–106; to rebellion and war, 34–35, 47–48, 51–52, 72, 87–88, 152; to withdrawal from public affairs, 26, 28, 29, 67, 70–72, 76, 77–78, 81, 130; examinations, 17, 20, 27, 33; FAMILY: aunt, 15, 22; brothers, 14, 52, 62–63, 73, 76, 94; children, 29, 43, 49–50, 53, 55–58, 77, 86, 87, 126; father, 14, 20, 22; grandfather, 14, 22; grandmother née Lu, 24; mother, 14–15; other relatives, 14–15, 18, 39, 42, 68, 88, 139; sister, 14, 52; wife, 43, 49–50, 55–58, 77, 86, 87; FEELINGS: for common people, 35–39, 44, 46, 64–66, 81–82, 88, 96–97, 109, 124–25, 151–52; for history, 13–14, 19; for horses, 21–22, 135–36, 141, 144; homesickness, 75, 89, 92, 129, 137; FRIENDSHIPS: *see* Cheng Ch'ien, Kao Shih, Li Po, Ts'en Shen, Su Yü, Wang Wei, poems of friendship; home at Yen-shih, 22, 33, 62, 68, 86, 92; influence on later poetry, 123, 134, 153–54; INTER-

EST: in military affairs, 14, 51–52, 60, 87, 90; in painting and calligraphy, 19, 133–40; in Taoism, 23; JOURNEYS: to Feng-hsien, 39, 40, 43; to Fu-chou from Feng-hsien, 49; to Feng-hsiang, 54; to Fu-chou from Ch'ang-an, 56; to Lo-yang, 62; to Ch'in-chou, 67; to T'ung-ku, 69; to Ch'eng-tu, 74; to Tzu-chou, 85–86; to Mien-chou, 86; to Han-chou, 86; to Lang-chou, 87; *see also* poems of travel, travels; marriage, 29; partisan of Fang Kuan, 55, 60, 62, 73, 86–87, 143; patrons, *see* Li Chin, Po Mao-lin, Wei Chi, Yen Wu; POEMS: allegorical, 73, 140–46; family, 43, 49–50, 55–58, 73; long, 74, 113, 120, 127; nature, 77, 120–23; war, 35–36, 51–52, 72–73, 87–88, 152; *yung-wu, see* allegorical; K'uei-chou period, 93, 94; Lung-yu period, 70; of friendship, 146–49; of recollection ᴀnd reminiscence, 94; of travel, 128–33; on hawks, 137–38; on horses, 135–36, 141, 144; on painting, 133–40; POSTS: quest for, 27–29, 32–33, 37, 40–42; police commissioner at Ho-hsi, 41; adjutant, 41; omissioner, 55; at Hua-chou, 62; military adviser to Yen Wu, 90; nominal Assistant Secretary of Ministry of Works, 90; poverty, 28–29, 37–39, 43, 69, 78–79, 101, 141; prisoner of rebels in Ch'ang-an, 49–54; sickness, 77, 78, 90, 92, 93; technique, 107–27; thatched hut, 75–80, 88–92; TRAVELS: in Wu and Yüeh, 17–20; in Ch'i and Chao, 17, 20; in Liang and Sung, 24; of last years, 95–97; twentieth-century evaluation, 150–54; wine and drinking, 16, 21, 25–26, 31, 42, 57, 61–62, 64, 78, 81, 105, 120, 122, 147

POEMS OF:

Abourd a Little Boat, 77; *Achieving a Poem While Drinking Alone,*

105; *At Random*, 80–81; *At the Sky's End Thinking of Li Po*, 74; *Autumn Thoughts*, 94, 113, 115–19; *Block the Lu-tzu Pass!*, 52; *Chance Topic*, 99–102; *Ch'iang Village, The*, 56–57; *Ch'eng-tu City*, 74–75; *Choosing a Dwelling*, 75, 77; *Cricket, The*, 142; *Curving Stream*, 61, 112; *Diseased Tangerines*, 81–82; *Doubt Me Not!*, 32, 90–91; *Dragon Gate Railed Way*, 133; *Dreaming of Li Po*, 147–48, 149; *Eight Laments*, 25, 31, 94; *Empty Purse, The*, 141; *Facing the Snow*, 52; *Feelings on Ancient Sites*, 94, 113–15; *Fire-fly, The*, 142; *Five Hundred Words to Express My Feelings When I Went from the Capital to Feng-hsien*, 40–41, 42, 43, 45, 111; *Flying Immortals Railed Way*, 132; *Four Pines, The*, 89; *Four Rhymes Again to Speed His Excellency Yen at Feng-chi Post Station*, 84; *Generals*, 94, 113; *Getting News of My Brothers*, 63; *Going Out of the Frontiers*, 35; *Hearing that the Imperial Armies Have Recovered Ho-nan and Ho-pei*, 86; *He Will Not Return*, 63; *Hsin-an Officer, The*, 65; *Hsüeh Chi's Painted Cranes on the Outside of the Wall of the T'ung-ch'üan Yamen*, 137; *Humorous Offering After the Post was Settled*, 41–42; *Hundred Anxieties*, 17, 78; *I Fell from a Horse When Drunk and My Friends Came to See Me, Bringing Wine*, 21–22; *I Have Become a Farmer*, 76; *I Have Not Seen . . .*, 148; *In the Moonlight of the Hundred and Fifth Night*, 43; *Journey North, The*, 57–59, 111, 129–31; *Keeping the Hua-men*, 151; *Lament by the River*, 53; *Lament for Ch'en-t'ao*, 51; *Lament for Ch'ing-fan*, 51; *Lament for a Prince*, 50; *Leaving Ch'in-chou*, 68; *Leaving T'ung-ku*, 69–70; *Lung-men*, 22–23; *Melon Frame, The*,

141–42; *Miscellaneous Poems of Ch'in-chou*, 68; *Missive to the Gentlemen of Hsien and Hua, A*, 109–10; *Moonlit Night*, 49–50, 112; *Moving to K'uei-chou*, 93; *Ni-kung Mountain*, 131; *On the River Encountering Waters Like the Sea, I Wrote a Short Poem on the Spot*, 102; *Past Excursion, A*, 34; *P'eng-ya Road*, 49, 111, 129, 130; *Playful Song for the Noble Hua*, 83; *Pounding Clothes*, 143; *Quatrain Sent to Kao Shih, Prefect of P'eng-chou Through Censor Ts'ui, A*, 79; *Quatrains*, 124–25; *Random Feelings*, 121–23; *Red Phoenix, The*, 144–45; *Rejoicing to have Reached the Traveling Court*, 54; *Remembering Li Po*, 147; *Remembering My Young Son*, 53; *Returning Geese*, 123–24; *Returning Swallows, The*, 143; *River Village, The*, 77; *River Village on a Spring Day, The*, 91; *Rotten Coir Palms*, 81, 82–83; *Secretary Wang Had Promised Money to Repair the Thatched Hut. Since It Had Not Arrived, I Sent a Small Reminder*, 123; *Seven Songs Written While Lodging at T'ung-ku*, 72; *Shih-hao Officer, The*, 66, 82; *Sick Horse, The*, 141; *Sighing on a Summer Day*, 67; *Sighing over the Autumn Rains*, 38; *Silkworms and Grain*, 97; *Six Quatrains Composed in Jest*, 106; *Song of the Ancient Cypress*, 110; *Song of the Bay from the Imperial Stables*, 135–36; *Song of Chiang Lord of Ch'u's Painting a Horned Hawk*, 137; *Song of the Cuckoo*, 145; *Song of the Eight Immortals of the Wine-cup*, 163; *Song of Fair Women*, 36, 110; *Song of the Firewood Carriers*, 109; *Song Inscribed in Jest on Wang Ts'ai's Landscape Painting*, 138–39; *Song of Li Ch'ao's Pa-fen and Small Seal Styles*, 139; *Song of My Nan Tree Uprooted by the Storm*, 79; *Song*

of My Thatched Roof Shattered by
the Autumn Wind, 79–80, 110;
Song of Painting: Presented to Gen-
eral Ts'ao Pa, 134–35; Song of the
Thin Horse, 144; Song of the War
Carts, 35–36, 50, 109, 152; Spending the Night at Headquarters, 90;
Spending the Night in the Pavilion
by the River, 94; Spring Yearning,
52, 112; Starting from Kung-an at
Dawn, 96; Temple of the Martial
Marquis, The, 123; Ten Rhymes to
Speed His Excellency Yen on His
Way to Court, 84; Thatched Hut,
The, 85, 88; Thinking of My Brothers, 63; Thinking of My Brothers on
a Moonlit Night, 73; Thirty
Rhymes to Hermit Chang Piao, 74,
104; Thoughts of a Night Traveler,
98; Three Officer (san-li) poems,
64–66, 112; Three Parting (san-
pieh) poems, 64, 112; To Be Inscribed On My Thatched Hut Beyond the River, 78, 89; To Describe
My Feelings, 55; To Dispel My
Grief, II, 20, VII, 103; To Express
My Feelings, 70–72; To Hermit
Chang, 25; To Li Po (chüeh-chü),
26, 119; To Li Po (wu-ku), 24; To
Scholars Ts'ui and Yü of the Chi-
hsien Yüan, 33; Traveling South,
97; Tree-bark Range, 132; Tsung-
wu's Birthday, 98; T'ung-kuan Officer, The, 65; Twenty-two Rhymes
to His Excellency Left Secretary
Wei, 27, 29–30, 34, 41, 104; Visitor, A, 78; Walking Alone Along
the River Bank to View the Blossoms, 120–21; Wanderings of My
Prime, The, 13, 16, 18, 19, 20, 21,
27, 31, 32, 111; Wash the Weapons
and the Horses!, 60; Written on the
day After the Beginning of
Autumn, 67; Yang Chien Also
Shows Me a Twelve-leaf Screen
Painted with Hawks, 137–38; Yang
Chien Shows Me a Piece of Chang
Hsü's Draft-Style, 139; Year is Ending, The, 96; poems: to his son Chi-
tzu, 126; to Kao Shih and Ts'en
Shen, 68, 74; to Recluse Wei, 63; to
Tu Kuan, 95; for Wei Yen's painting, 136

OTHER WRITING OF:

Fu on the Three Great Ceremonies,
32, 33; sacrificial pieces: for Fang
Kuan, 87; for Tu Yü, 13; tomb
inscriptions: for his aunt, 15, 22;
for his step-grandmother, 14

Tu Hsien, 14, 20, 22
Tu Kuan, 94
Tu-ling, 15, 34, 40
T'ung-ch'üan, 137
T'ung-ku, 69, 74, 131
T'ung-kuan, 47, 48, 55, 65, 130
Tung-men Hills, 26
Tung-t'ing Lake, 96, 97, 139
Turks, 15, 20
Tu Shen-yen, 14, 22
Tu Tso, 68
Tu Village, 15, 33–34
Tu Wei, 42
Tu Yü, 13, 22
Tzu-chou, 78, 83, 85, 86

Uighurs, 50–51, 86, 151
"unicorns" (horses), 136

Vermilion Terrace, 135
Vimalakirti, 19

Wa-kuan monastery, 19
Waley, Arthur, 146
Wang, Prefect of Lang-chou, 87
Wang Chao-chün, 109, 114
Wang family, 19
Wang Fu, 100
Wang Han, 30
Wang Hsi-chih (Right General Wang),
134, 139
Wang Liang, 136
Wang P'o, 106
Wang Ts'ai, 138
Wang Ts'an, 92, 95, 100
Wang Wei, 59, 107, 119, 133, 138, 149

Wang-wu shan, 24
Water Gate (at K'uei-chou), 94
Weaving Girl, 43, 118
Wei (recluse), 63
Wei (river), 30, 38, 63
Wei, Madam (Wei Shuo), 134
Wei Chi, 27, 28, 29–30, 34
Wei Ch'i-hsin, 16
Wei Yen, 136
Wen (founder of Chou dynasty), 115
Wen-tzu, 23
Western Palace, 145
Western Range, 124
West Pavilion (at K'uei-chou), 93–94
White Emperor's City (K'uei-chou), 21, 93, 116
White Pavilion (at Ch'ang-an), 102
Wordsworth, 154
Wu, Emperor of Han, 117, 118
Wu Gorge, 111, 115
Wu Hills, 109
Wu-kung, 54
Wu-men, 34
Wu-sung River, 139
Wu T'ai-po, 19
Wu-wei (border command), 41

Yang Chien, 137, 139
Yang Ch'iung, 106
Yang-chou, 20
Yang family, 36
Yang family (imperial of Sui dynasty), 15

Yang Hsiung, 16, 29, 76
Yang Kuei-fei, 36, 45, 48, 53
Yang Kuo-chung, 36–37, 47, 48
Yang T'ai-chen. *See* Yang Kuei-fei
Yangtse (Kiang), 18 *et passim*
Yangtse Gorges (Three Gorges), 93, 113, 114
Yao-niao (horse), 136
Yeh, 59, 62, 66, 73
Yeh, (capital of Wei dynasty), 100
Yeh-lang, 60
Yellow River (the Ho), 18 *et passim*
Yen-an, 52
Yen-chou, 14, 20, 24, 25
Yen-en kuei ("Favor-Inviting Box"), 32
Yen-shih, 22, 33, 62, 68, 86, 89, 92
Yen Wu, 60, 62, 73, 84, 85, 86, 88, 90, 92–93
Ying Ch'ang, 100
Yin K'eng, 26, 103
"Young Wife's Memorial," 100
Yu ("secret beauty"), 77
Yüan, Emperor of Han, 114
Yüan Chen, 13, 146, 154
Yüan Chieh, 27, 98
Yüan Hsien, 30
Yu-chi (travel records), 129
Yü-chou, 93
Yüeh-chou, 96
Yüeh-fu, 112, 143, 148
Yü Hsin, 100, 101, 106, 113, 147
Yün-an, 93
Yung-an Palace, 114